A KINDRED ORPHANHOOD

A KINDRED ORPHANHOOD

❖

Sergey Gandlevsky

❖

translated from the Russian
by PHILIP METRES

ZEPHYR PRESS
Brookline, MA

Cover photograph of Sergey Gandlevsky by Roman Spektor
Book design by *typeslowly*
Printed in Canada

Zephyr Press acknowledges with gratitude the financial support
of The Tiny Tiger Foundation, Charles Merrill, and the Massachusetts
Cultural Council.

MASSACHUSETTS CULTURAL COUNCIL

Library of Congress Control Number: 2003111573

07 06 05 04 03   98765432 FIRST EDITION

ZEPHYR PRESS
50 Kenwood Street
Brookline, MA 02446
www.zephyrpress.org

Acknowledgments

My deep gratitude to Sergey Gandlevsky for his generosity and patience. Special thanks to Dmitry Psurtsev for his mentoring, consultation on annotation, and advice on translating; simply put, without Dima, this book would not exist. Thanks to Amy Breau, for her encouragement, support, and always careful reading. Thanks as well to Jessica Baldanzi, Daniel Bourne, Jim Doppke, Chris Green, Jim Kates, Lev Loseff, Cris Mattison, Kay Metres, E.J. McAdams, Philip Nikolayev and Rasul Shafikov. The following journals and anthologies have published versions of these translations:

Artful Dodge: "To land a job at the garage," "Oh, the lilacs this May!" "It's time to change the record," and "December 1977"
Asheville Poetry Review: "To. E.F. Fadeeva"
Combo: "The lynch law of sudden maturity"
Exquisite Corpse: "Stanzas," "Struck down with this illness," and "To My Wife"
Field: "To Pavel Movchan (Outside Chernobyl)"
Fulcrum: "Everyone knows how thunder comes," "The chatter of daws," and "I'll kiss your shining sinful forehead"
Glas: New Russian Writing: "Long ago, we wandered in on the festival of death," "In the beginning of December, when nature dreams," and "The lynch law of sudden maturity"
In the Grip of Strange Thoughts: Russian Poetry in a New Era: "Oh, the lilacs this May!" "It's time to change the record," "To E.F. Fadeeva," "Dear God, allow me to recall my works," and "Here is our street, let's say"
Mid-American Review chapbook: "The communal zoo quieted," "Twice, last night, I dreamt," "There are nights," and the essay "The Use of Poetry"
Modern Poetry in Translation: "Twilight came late"
New Orleans Review: "Here rivers cry," and "Semyon Kosikh"
Przeklandiec: "When a middle-aged man"
Rhino: "To O.E."
Seneca Review: "*Look, it's snowing again*"
Tin House: "To My Mother"
Willow Springs: "Here is our street, let's say" and "Elegy"

Table of Contents

The Generation of Nightwatchmen: Sergey Gandlevsky and Underground Poetry During the Soviet Stagnation

Sergey Markovich Gandlevsky was born in Moscow in 1952, one year before Stalin's death. An integral figure in the Seventies Generation, Gandlevsky was one of the underground Russian poets who wrote only for themselves and their friends during the Brezhnev era. Gandlevsky began writing too late to enjoy the Thaw, that mid-60s moment of cultural freedom, when Yevtushenko, Vosnesensky, and Akhmadulina recited their poems to packed stadiums. When the Thaw ended in 1968 with the brutal Soviet crackdown in Prague, the stadium poets—who continued to receive the privileges accorded to members of the Writers Union—lost much of their credibility in the eyes of the younger generation. In the words of Andrew Wachtel and Aleksei Parschikov, the poetic stars of the Sixties generation "came to symbolize complete capitulation to the new order."

Despite their relative cultural obscurity—or perhaps, precisely because of their situation as internal émigrés— Gandlevsky and the Seventies Generation forged new directions in Russian poetry (often reasserting links to previous generations of underground poets), less fettered by the political pressures on Russian writers both prior to, and during, the Soviet period. Indeed, continuing an unbroken tradition of Russian intellectuals and artists, hundreds of kitchen tables, rather than the stadium, were the islands of an invisible cultural archipelago. By the 1980s, poetry circles and poetry clubs, according to literary critic Lena Trofimova, "began to arise and disseminate in the theater studios, state literary clubs and associations connected with writing." Wachtel and Parschikov explain that "this concept of small group society was not limited to the poets of the underground; it was a characteristic model for Soviet life in this period in general, and for intellectual life in particular."

At Moscow State University, Gandlevsky helped found one of the crucial groups, "Moscow Time," which included fellow comrade-poets Aleksander Soprovsky, Aleksey Tsvetkov, and Bakhyt Kenjeev, among others. Trofimova recalls how Moscow Time's "poetic fraternity opposed the official literary studio of the university, who had all the necessities of a comfortable but a conformist existence—good lodging, financial support, organized regulations of study." And yet, far from seeing themselves as political dissidents, Gandlevsky and Moscow Time actually felt honored to, in his words, "bridle [our] desire to be printed. For us, literature was a private matter.... There was no one whose eyes needed to be opened, who needed to be convinced."

Gandlevsky, like many of the underground, chose unprestigious careers or odd jobs, both to avoid participating in what he saw as a morally bankrupt society, and to free up time for writing and travel. For Gandlevsky, to work was to collaborate with the system that was committing autogenocide. Gandlevsky recalled to Masha Gessen how his circle suffered from an "honesty psychosis":

> We were constantly taking things apart into what's honest and what's not, like medieval priests struggling to figure out how many angels can dance on the head of a pin. To work is to participate, which is dishonest, but to work as a night [watchman] making 70 roubles a month—that seems honest because you can't make any less and we don't want to kill ourselves ... And most of all, we had this weary attitude toward speech, as toward a person who had been caught stealing.

Gandlevsky worked as an English literature teacher, museum docent, theater stagehand, and night watchman. Relying on samizdat (self-publishing), Gandlevsky and other poets of the underground did not appear in Russian literary journals until the late 1980s. Since then, Gandlevsky has become one of the most important contemporary Russian poets, in 1996 winning both the Little Booker Prize and the

Anti-Booker Prize for a volume of his selected poems and a memoir, *Trepanation of the Skull*, respectively. While he continues to write poetry, he has expanded his repertoire into drama, critical essay, and, most recently, a novel. His work has been translated into numerous languages and has been included in nearly every major English translation anthology of Russian, including *20th Century Russian Poetry: Silver and Steel* (Doubleday Press, 1993), *The Third Wave* (University of Michigan Press, 1992), and *In the Grip of Strange Thoughts: Russian Poetry in a New Era* (Zephyr Press, 1999).

If the affiliations of the Seventies Generation provide a cultural context of the "stagnation period," they do not suffice to tell Gandlevsky's story. Mikhail Aizenberg, a poet and friend of Gandlevsky's, has remarked, quite rightly, how "all those who lived in the 'underground world' were lone riders, outsiders. I mean precisely 'outsiders,' and not 'members of the opposition'; they did not stand against any one thing in particular, but against everything at the same time. There could not have been a worse position for creating a group."

Even without the institutional constraints placed on Soviet poets, Gandlevsky wrote in strict form, what Russian poetry terms "classical form." Gandlevsky once said that classical form was "given to me by birth ... there really wasn't any choice for me in this regard." Though a few examples of experimental verse like Mayakovsky's were available, Gandlevsky's persistent use of classical form suggests his longing for connection to a Russian poetic tradition that had been buried by Soviet imperatives, one which Mandelstam dreamed would be part of a great world culture. Gandlevsky has also suggested that "the effect of my poems, if it exists, partially comes from the convergence of classical, almost sculptural form and everyday content." That convergence of high cultural formalism and low cultural content creates what Aizenberg has called the "explosive mixture" of Gandlevsky's verse.

How to translate this explosivity? How to translate that tension, both classically situated and yet linguistically adrift? It is by now a translator's cliché to evoke the pliability and richness of the Russian language. The regularity of Russian conjugations and declensions, the flexibility of word order in sentence meaning, and the multisyllabic nature of Russian words all combine to create a seemingly endless wellspring of rhymes and metrical possibilities. Precisely because regular rhyme and meter is still almost completely the norm in Russian poetry, Gandlevsky's use of everyday, even vulgar language challenges the very definitions of the poem as a beautiful or pure utterance. Because, to the American taste weaned on free verse, formalist verse can veer towards artificiality—an effect that would belie Gandlevsky's naturalism—I have chosen to translate Gandlevsky into what Antony Easthope terms "intonational meter," with particular attention to the muscularity of the line. Tone, in American poetry perhaps since Whitman, is itself a kind of form, structured around the experience of breath, phrasing, and the illusion of coherent voice. In general, I lean toward the natural iambs of the English language, while relying on slant and true rhymes to ghost the original, without breaking the spell of intonation.

Gandlevsky packs traditional poetic forms with, on the one hand, numerous literary references (Pushkin, Lermontov, Blok, Mandelstam, Pasternak, Nabokov, Goethe), and on the other, with Soviet-era slang, soap brands, and pop bands. Andrew Wachtel has suggested that many poets of Gandlevsky's generation mirror the work of the New York School and of pop artists like Warhol and Lichtenstein, "in their more complex gestures to bracket mass culture in ironic or parodic terms." Gandlevsky has whimsically termed his style "critical sentimentalism," an oxymoronic category that melds the high odic style of classical literature with the low ironic style of postmodern writing. Echoing Russian poets such as Vladislav Khodasevich, Georgy Ivanov, and Lev Loseff, Gandlevsky's poems explore cynicism, sentimentality, self-loathing and disdain. Reminiscent of Robert Lowell's work, whose confessional poems of mania seethe under the hard artifice of form and allusion, Gandlevsky's poetry works precisely through yoking oppositions—between form and content, between high concerns and daily indignities. So while traditional themes of poetry emerge from his work—obsession with language, freedom, death, love, the muse—these concerns always emerge against the backdrop of a life full of personal and social vulgarities: militarism, alcoholism, debauchery, ennui.

This book is the first English translation of poems by Gandlevsky, and roughly follows Gandlevsky's chronological order, partly because it so clearly documents not only his own journey, or even just the journey of the underground, but also the journey of a nation. According to Chris Green, Gandlevsky "seems to have lived by poetry, as if it were a raft to swim through the last twenty-five years of Soviet history."

The opening poem "Stanzas" is Gandlevsky's *ars poetica*. Written in 1987, on the edge of tumultuous changes in Russian society, "Stanzas" is a poet's conversation with himself, cajoling himself to speak, but not completely convinced that he has a subject worthy of poetry:

> Speak. But what do you want to say? Perhaps
> How the barge moved along the city river, trailing sunset,
> How for two-thirds of June until the solstice
> Summer stretched on its tiptoes to the light,
> How breath of linden blew through sultry squares
> And how thunder rolled from all directions that July?
> You once believed that speech needs an underlying cause
> And a grave occasion. But that's a lie.

In a poem that contains an hourglass, a Rubik's Cube, static electricity, downers, and workers drinking beer, Gandlevsky sings the mundane, not out of a Whitmanesque expansion of the spirit, but to answer the voice that hurts him into speech. Between nostalgia and cynicism, Gandlevsky lurches through the landscape, ridiculing himself as a "haggard charlatan" unable to take a simple snapshot. In the end, he imagines himself after death, outside Moscow, where he will "lift [his] snout to sky, throw back [his] antlers," trumpeting "what human words could not express."

Gandlevsky's early poems gyre further and further from Moscow, until he finds himself at the edges of the Soviet empire, at the edges of his own language. In the densely allusive poem, "Here rivers cry like a patient under the knife," he acknowledges how his metaphors somehow fail to describe the rivers, as "they keen/A dialect one hundred times/More strange." Among the mountains, where not even Russian history has permeated, Gandlevsky enjoins, even as he writes:

Conceited poetry, hide the notepad:
There are places in the world beyond
Our words—and we cannot understand,
Can't translate, the Pamir's husky tongue.

In these lines, Gandlevsky acknowledges that language is always translation, and that poetry's overweening confidence can be imperial in its yearnings. Like many of his generation, Gandlevsky, even while an inhabitant at the center of empire, follows the inner centrifugal forces away from power, as if he can thrive only by physically departing from the ideological confidence of Moscow.

Gandlevsky's poetry often works through what Robert Bly termed "leaping poetry"—that associative movement that defies surface rationality and works through a submerged, even unconscious logic. These leaps, like the cinematic techniques of splicing and panning, enable Gandlevsky's poems to span time and space far beyond the traditional lyric. And yet, far from yielding an ecstatic vision of union, these leaps frequently give way to a foreboding sense of the apocalypse. In "Twice, last night, I dreamt," his dream of a car accident and the death of his mother suddenly becomes a movie he's watching in a village club, where "the projectionist's always drunk," and where the speakers don't work. He leaps, suddenly, to imagining the end of suffering, which is the end of the world, when "we will be washed from the canvas screen." In 1977, it is as if Gandlevsky already senses that these are the twilight years of the Soviet empire. Some ten years later, in "To Pavel Movchan," Gandlevsky would write about the Chernobyl incident, which many people believed to be a sign of the end of the world.

Gandlevsky's world-weariness is masculine, and his poems occasionally perform a wounded bravado, an over-inflated machismo. But just as the American confessional poets often play with the ruse of unmasking, Gandlevsky's poems are not simple autobiographical confessions. Gandlevsky once said that though his poems "underline the biographical," his memory "is cunning, not simple-hearted, and very selective." Not surprisingly, in a persona poem like "To land a job at the garage," a sense of self-accusation and guilt weighs down the poem, and belies any simplistic reading. Echoing the song "Bolshoi Karetny" by Vladimir Vysotsky, the speaker of the poem brags of sexual conquests and failed responsibilities:

> To land a job at the garage
> And sing about a black pistol.
> And not once in ten years
> Stop and visit your old mother.
> En route from Gazli in the south
> After a canister of sour wine
> Screw some girlfriend in Kaluga,
> Leave her when she's pregnant.
> Gaseteria lamb on Wednesdays,
> Cod-pea soup on Thursdays.
> To vow to a friend at lunch
> To rough up a garage owner, then
> Surmount the promising crest
> Of a thirtieth birthday…

Gandlevsky's relentlessly documentary mode grips onto the margins of the Soviet Union—(Gazli is in Uzbekistan)—and also to everyday objects—the "canister of sour wine." He forces a translator to scramble between retaining cultural particulars, at the risk of losing the American reader, and opting for some American equivalences, at the risk of effacing the original contexts. (Looking for the American equivalent of "rygalovka," a Gandlevskian neologism combining the words "to belch" and "diner," on a bus ride from Boston to New York, I found it. Somewhere around 125ᵗʰ Street, I looked up and saw: "Gaseteria.")

To read poems like "To land a job at the garage," "Dear God, allow me to recall my works," and "To E.F. Fadeeva" is to feel Gandlevsky's spiritual (though not formal) connection to Beat poets like Allen Ginsberg, Jack Kerouac, Bob Dylan. These are poems of the road, hard-traveling and longing for a home; poems of drinking in the morning to relieve a hangover; poems of wounded machismo and tenderness, of cynicism and sentimentalism; poems of defiance, lifting the dead weight of a Molochian system from one's chest with rhyme; poems that view Russia with the gaze of an outsider, unhoused and restless in the gigantism of Moscow and the outskirts of the empire, "from Omsk to Osh."

Gandlevsky's spiritual quest might evoke images of the Beats for the American reader, but for the Russian reader, one hears the keen sounds of Russia's long poetic and literary tradition. When Gandlevsky quipped in an interview, "my homeland is Russian literature," he was simultaneously describing his status as an inner exile and quoting Korolenko. When reading Gandlevsky, a Russian reader might hear, depending on the poem, Pushkin's measured lyric delight in the natural world; Chekhov's alternating atmospheres of gloom and grace; Blok's foreboding symbolism; Mandelstam's dark paranoiac urgency of the Voronezh years; Okudzhava's light melancholy songs of Old Arbat; Vysotsky's gutteral vocalizations of alcoholism and travel; or Nabokov's plaintive nostalgia for the lost Russia of his childhood. Gandlevsky's conversation—at times, his argument—with tradition is something that we may only vaguely discern, just ghostly demarcations. Still, even for the Russian reader, Gandlevsky's poetry does not politely invoke the great writers, but rather brings them alive to interrogate them, as if to ask: what help can you bring us now?

The sense of time passing—of an era, of the lives around the poet, of his own life—pervades the poems. He laments the passing of his childhood communal apartment in "The communal zoo," and in poems like "In the beginning of December" and "Elegy" he confronts the transience of existence itself. The final poems, written when Gandlevsky learned he had a brain tumor, have an unsparing, brutal edge. He describes in one poem, before surgery, "a loud ticking, everywhere," as if the tumor itself were a time bomb. In a book haunted by muses, this final muse offers no easy answers, just "words you can't quite read."

Having interviewed numerous Russian poets while living in Moscow, I chose to translate Gandlevsky because he captured the spirit of his time more scrupulously, more intensely, than any other poet of his generation. By 1992, Gandlevsky was editing the journal *Foreign Literature* and raising his children Sasha and Grisha with his wife, Lena, a sculptor. Walking with his boxer Charlie through the crooked streets of Moscow, Gandlevsky stopped short and pointed to the roof of a crumbling monastery. It was here, some years ago, he recalled, he once shared a bottle of vodka with a drinking buddy. Those days, the days of the kitchen archipelago, are gone. We returned to his apartment and watched "The Blues Brothers" dubbed in Russian. I tried to explain the significance of John Lee Hooker; he nodded, understanding something beyond my ability to explain.

In poetic translation, the muse is not always a wispy wraith, but sometimes a grizzled veteran of brain surgery and the bottle. While living in Moscow, I remember telling a Russian friend that I was learning more about myself—about my limitations, my cultural blindnesses—than I was about Russia and Russian culture. It saddened him. Living in another country, living in another language and culture does indeed tell us much about ourselves. But it does more than this. It calls us to reach outside of ourselves and the horizons of our experience into the unknown, and into what cannot be known. And yet, moments of connection occur, sometimes when we least expect it. The surprise in instinctively understanding a turn of phrase, or in speaking it ourselves. The delight in reaching across the abyss of language into another person's world. Understanding a line of poetry, and realizing that this has become your country, that you share, in Gandlevsky's words, "a kindred orphanhood."

Philip Metres

Fathoming Gandlevsky

LEV LOSEFF

Epicurus, Bentham, Freud, et al., were right: the goal of life is pleasure, and when we open a volume of Sergey Gandlevsky's poems, this goal is achieved.

It is easier to say what Gandlevsky's poetry is not. It has little in common with the breathtaking intellectual and metaphysical vistas of Joseph Brodsky. Its casual intonation and pedestrian phraseology are the total opposite of Marina Tsvetaeva's ecstatic verse and the verbal magic of Osip Mandelstam. These are what-you-see-is-what-you-get poems, unlike the deceptively simple poems of Anna Akhmatova, which she herself compared to boxes with secret compartments. Gandlevsky's poetry bears some resemblance to that of Boris Pasternak—not young Pasternak, the impetuous metaphorizer, but old Pasternak, the Zhivago poet—and yet the resemblance is superficial. Both explore routine, daily life for lyrical potential but their inspiration is different. Pasternak is on a mission: he strives to transform daily life along the lines of Christian mystery. Gandlevsky takes it as it is.

But what is it?

There were places on Earth where human misery presented itself in sharp contrast to a magnificently colorful natural environment—in Africa, Southeast Asia, or Central America. A quick trip from Park Avenue in Manhattan to the South Bronx could be as dramatic as Orpheus' descent to Hades. Conflict, contrast, and collision give impetus to poetic imagination. But what would you do out of entropy? The common color of the country, which for three-quarters of the last century called itself "Red Russia," was gray. Gray were the bulky clothes of women in foodlines. Gray were the faces of their sons and husbands, as were the faces of people who just returned from prison, or after an eight-hour shift at a chemical plant. Cheap vodka in transparent bottles looked gray when shared hurriedly under the ever-bleak northern sky, among dilapidated concrete tenements.

Gandlevsky turns the monotony and squalor of Soviet/post-Soviet life into lyrical poetry of the highest probe, and the means by which he achieves it are utterly minimalist. If one has a dream in his poem, it is a dream about fixing an old shed and not having matches to light a cigarette. His diction is almost as mumbling and cliché-ridden as a conversation in a crowded commuter train. His verse forms strictly adhere to the versification rules of a middle-school textbook: iambic pentameter or iambic hexameter for meditative poems, anapest for more sentimental lines. Yet, I repeat, nothing finds a more direct way to your heart than these flotsam and jetsam of the commonplace carried by regular iambic or anapestic waves.

I will attempt to divine the secret of Gandlevsky's irresistible lyric by commenting in a detached "classroom" manner on one poem, "To Alexander Magarik."

The poem is short—4 eight-line stanzas, i.e., about average size for Gandlevsky. The lines are alternately anapestic tetrameter and trimeter with correspondingly alternating feminine and masculine rhymes. In music a rhythmical counterpart to this pattern would be a waltz, the preferred form of old sentimental songs. Indeed, the love for unpretentious sentimental songs, which the author shares with Russian ordinary folks, seems to be the theme of the poem.

The poem begins as a request for a song after another round of drinks, which is followed by a hint at the unabashed emoting required for singing such a song:

Sing something about prison and parting,
With tears and a mouth full of foam.
Something from Kostroma or Velikie Luki
But when drinking, something about the gulag.

The author proposes a typical plot from a jailbird's repertoire:

> This song's about how a son finally came home
> On medical leave, his hair gone white.
> He drank at Ninka's, cried at Klavka's—
> My God, my God, have you forgiven us?

At this point, as if overwhelmed by emotion, he interrupts himself with his exclamation. (Note: not a hint of irony in all that).

The first six lines of the second stanza are a sketch of a train station:

> Our train station, visible for miles around:
> A gutter lisping to itself,
> Someone singing of platform farewells,
> Of hooligans taken to the east.
> Of people, bread, strategic cargo
> Traveling the homeland all day.
> A song about wasted life—
> I'm not particular, just play.

While the poet was directly addressing the singers in the first stanza, here he looks at them from afar. For a while I could not understand why I saw the weather in this picture as wet. Now I realize: the "lisping" drain! In the two concluding lines—"Something about wasted life—I'm not particular, just play" Gandlevsky suddenly returns to the speech, which was interrupted at the end of the first stanza, to addressing somebody with a request for a heart-rending song, but . . .

The third stanza is clearly self-addressed, and includes a splendid metaphor which no teetotaler could ever appreciate:

> In the fall, go out to the open fields,
> Cool your head in homeland wind.
> A gulp of alcohol is like a hot rose,
> Unfolding in your chest.

The third stanza ends in "as if"—"you breathe as if"—rushing us to the last stanza, where we find ourselves within the jail song:

> You woke to an overcast dawn …
> The door clangs, the gruel's brought in,
> You brush off your foolish hopes
> And are taken in your underwear. In the distance,

This enjambment signifies another switch in the plane of vision. Or does it? Isn't the view presented in the four ending lines—what the poor guy in the song is seeing while being taken away in his underwear? He sees

> A pond is covered in gooseflesh,
> A semaphore forces itself to shine,
> Rain scatters down, and an unshaven man
> Talks to himself as he passes by.

Such is the Moebius strip of one of Gandlevsky's lyrical plots: near a train station on a cold and wet day, the poet asks for a folk song, becomes the doomed hero of the song and, finally, looks through the eyes of this hero at himself, who is creating this very poem on a wet and cold day, near a train station.

His means are minimalist, but the effect wrenches your heart.

A Kindred Orphanhood

СТАНСЫ

Памяти матери

I.
Говори. Что ты хочешь сказать? Не о том ли, как шла
Городскою рекою баржа по закатному следу,
Как две трети июня, до двадцать второго числа,
Встав на цыпочки, лето старательно тянется к свету,
Как дыхание липы сквозит в духоте площадей,
Как со всех четырех сторон света гремело в июле?
А что речи нужна позарез подоплека идей
И нешуточный повод - так это тебя обманули.

II.

Слышишь: гнилью арбузной пахнул овощной магазин,
За углом в подворотне грохочет порожняя тара,
Ветерок из предместий донес перекличку дрезин,
И архивной листвою покрылся асфальт тротуара.
Урони кубик Рубика наземь, не стоит труда,
Все расчеты насмарку, поешь на дожде винограда,
Сидя в тихом дворе, и воочью увидишь тогда,
Что приходит на память в горах и расщелинах ада.

III.

И иди, куда шел. Но, как в бытность твою по ночам,
И особенно в дождь, будет голою веткой упрямо,
Осязая оконные стекла, программный анчар
Трогать раму, что мыла в согласии с азбукой мама.
И хоть уровень школьных познаний моих невысок,
Вижу как наяву: сверху вниз сквозь отверстие в колбе
С приснопамятным шелестом сыпался мелкий песок.
Немудрящий прибор, но какое раздолье для скорби!

Stanzas

—In Memory of My Mother

I.

Speak. But what do you want to say? Perhaps
How the barge moved along the city river, trailing sunset,
How all June until the solstice
Summer stretched on its tiptoes to the light,
How breath of linden blew through sultry squares
And how thunder rolled from all directions that July?
You once believed that speech needs an underlying cause
And a grave occasion. But that's a lie.

II.

Listen: the grocery store reeks of watermelon rot,
An empty crate clatters at a back door around the corner.
From the suburbs, a breeze carries the echo of a handcar
And buries the asphalt in archive leaves.
Drop the Rubik's Cube to the ground—it's not worth the trouble.
When all plans fail, eat grapes in the rain,
Sit in the silent yard. Just look with your own eyes.
This is what you'll recall among the crags and crevices of hell—

III.

So get going. Yet a naked branch—the upas
Of school texts—stubbornly touches the window
Just as it did long ago, at night, especially during rain,
Feeling the pane that mama washed.
Though I remember very little from school
I can still see each grain of sand pouring through
The narrow glass neck, an unforgettable rustle.
A primitive instrument, but what a throat for sorrow!

IV.

Об пол злостью, как тростью, ударь, шельмовства не тая,
Испитой шарлатан с неизменною шаткой треногой,
Чтоб прозрачная призрачная распустилась струя
И озоном запахло под жэковской кровлей убогой.
Локтевым электричеством мебель ужалит - и вновь
Говори, как под пыткой, вне школы и без манифеста,
Раз тебе, недобитку, внушают такую любовь
Это гиблое время и Богом забытое место.

V.

В это время вдовец Айзенштадт, сорока семи лет,
Колобродит по кухне и негде достать пипольфена.
Есть ли смысл веселиться, приятель, я думаю, нет,
Даже если он в траурных черных трусах до колена.
В этом месте, веселье которого есть питие,
За порожнею тарой видавшие виды ребята
За Серегу Есенина или Андрюху Шенье
По традиции пропили очередную зарплату.

VI.

После смерти я выйду за город, который люблю,
И, подняв к небу морду, рога запрокинув на плечи,
Одержимый печалью, в осенний простор протрублю
То, на что не хватило мне слов человеческой речи.
Как баржа уплывала за поздним закатным лучом,
Как скворчало железное время на левом запястье,
Как заветную дверь отпирали английским ключом …
Говори. Ничего не поделаешь с этой напастью.

1987

IV.

Strike spitefully on the floor your ever-wobbly tripod,
Haggard charlatan, not hiding your crookedness,
So that a clear specter of water streams out, smells of ozone
Under the leaking roof of a state-owned house.
The chair jolts you with static electricity,
So speak again, as if tortured, sans schools and manifestoes,
If this hopeless time and god-forsaken place
Instill in you, a total deadbeat, such love.

V.

The widower, forty-seven year old Aizenstadt
Now roams the kitchen, can't cop his usual downer.
Is there reason to smile at this, my friend? I think not.
Even if his funeral-black boxers hang down to his knees.
In this world, where one needs spirits to be happy,
Behind empty crates the guys who've seen better days
Raise a toast to Sergey Esenin or Andy Chenier,
Squander their latest check on drink by tradition.

VI.

After death I'll go to the outskirts of the city I love,
Lift my snout to sky, throw back my antlers—
Taken by sadness, I'll trumpet into autumn space
What human words could not express.
How the barge sailed into the wake of sunsetting day,
How iron time on my left wrist sang like a starling,
How the secret door was unlocked with a house key.
Speak. There's nothing else you can do with this affliction.

ДЕКАБРЬ 1977 ГОДА

Штрихи и точки нотного письма.
Кленовый лист на стареньком пюпитре.
Идет смычок, и слышится зима.
Ртом горьким улыбнись и слезы вытри,
Здесь осень музицирует сама.
Играй, октябрь, зажмурься, не дыши.
Вольно мне было музыке не верить,
Кощунствовать, угрюмо браконьерить
В скрипичном заповеднике души.
Вольно мне очутиться на краю
И музыку, наперсницу мою, -
Все тридцать три широких оборота -
Уродовать семьюдестью восьмью
Вращениями хриплого фокстрота.
Условимся о гибели молчать.
В застолье нету места укоризне
И жалости. Мне скоро двадцать пять,
Мне по карману праздник этой жизни.
Холодные созвездия горят.
Глухого мирозданья не корят
Остывшие Ока, Шексна и Припять.
Поэтому я предлагаю выпить
За жизнь с листа и веру наугад.
За трепет барабанных перепонок.
В последний день, когда меня спросонок
По имени окликнут в тишине,
Неведомый пробудится ребенок
И втайне затоскует обо мне.
Условимся о гибели молчок.
Нам вечность беззаботная не светит.
А если кто и выронит смычок,
То музыка сама себе ответит.

1977

December 1977

The strokes and notes of a musical script,
A maple leaf on an old music stand.
The bow moves, and winter begins to sound.
So grin bitterly, wipe away your tears,
Autumn performs its song alone.
Play, October, with eyes closed, not breathing.
It was my choice not to believe in music,
To blaspheme, to poach sullenly
In the violin preserve of the soul.
It was my choice to end up at the edge
And mutilate music, my confidante—
All thirty-three wide turns—
The rotations of a hoarse fox trot
At the speed of a seventy-eight.
Let's keep quiet about dying.
At the table there's no place for reproach
Or pity. I'll soon be twenty-five.
I can afford this celebration of life.
The cold constellations shine.
The bracing Oka, Sheksna, Pripyat rivers
Don't rebuke the deaf universe.
So I propose a toast to life
Played off the page, to an accidental belief.
To the trembling of eardrums.
On the last day, when, still groggy,
In the silence I'm called by name,
An unknown child will struggle to waken
And begin secretly to long for me.
Let's agree, not a word about dying.
Easy immortality is not in our future.
Yet if someone happens to drop a bow,
Then the music, by itself, will answer.

✧✧✧

Мы знаем приближение грозы,
Бильярдного раскатистого треска -
Позвякивают ведра и тазы,
Кликушествует злая занавеска.
В такую ночь в гостинице меня
Оставил сон и вынудил к беседе
С самим собой. Педалями звеня,
Горбун проехал на велосипеде
В окне моем. Я не зажег огня.
Блажен, кто спит. Я встал к окну спиной.
Блажен, кто спит в разгневанном июле.
Я в сумерки вгляделся - предо мной
Сиделкою душа спала на стуле.
Давно ль, скажи, ты девочкой была?
Давно ль провинциалкой босоногой
Ступни впервые резала осокой,
И плакала, и пела? Но сдала
И, сидя, спишь в гостинице убогой.
Морщинки. Рта порочные углы.
Тяжелый сон. Виски в капели пота.
И страшно стало мне в коробке мглы -
Ужели это все моя работа!
С тех пор боюсь: раскаты вдалеке
Поднимут за полночь настойчиво и сухо -
На стуле спит усталая старуха
С назойливою мухой на щеке.
Я закричу, умру - горбун в окне,
Испуганная завесь ворвется.
Душа вздрогнёт, медлительно очнется,
Забудет все, отдаст усталость мне
И девочкой к кому-нибудь вернется.

1976

❖❖❖

Everyone knows how thunder comes—
The resonant billiard-crack, then
The ringing of buckets and wash-basins,
The ominous prophecy of angry curtains.
On such a night in a hotel, sleep
Deserted me and forced a conversation
With myself. A hunchback
Rode a bicycle, pedals clanking,
Across my window. I didn't turn on the light.
Blessed is the sleeper. I stood up.
Blessed is he who can sleep in furious July.
I peered into the gloom. Before me,
Like a nurse, the soul asleep on a stool.
Tell me, how long since you were a girl?
How long since you, barefoot provincial,
First cut your foot on sharp sedge,
And cried, then sang? But you succumbed to age,
And sitting, you sleep in this squalid hotel.
Wrinkles, distorted corners of your mouth.
Deep in dream. Sweat dripping down temples.
And I became afraid in this dark box—
Perhaps this was all my fault.
Since then I've feared distant thunder
Rousing after midnight, urgent and dry—
The weary old woman sleeping on a chair,
A persistent fly at her cheek. I'll cry out,
I'll die—a hunchback in the window,
The frightened curtain bursting in.
The soul will shudder, sluggishly re-awaken,
Forget everything, give back my weariness
And return, a girl again, to someone else.

И.Б.

Бывают вечера - шатается под ливнем
Трава, и слышен водосточный хрип.
Легко бродить и маяться по длинным
Аллеям монастырских лип.

Сквозь жизнь мою доносится удушье
Московских лип, и хочется в жилье,
Где ты марала ватман черной тушью,
И начиналось прошлое мое.

Дитя надменное с этюдником отцовским,
Скажи, едва ли ни вчера
Нам по арбатским кухням стариковским
Кофейник звякал до утра?

Нет, я не о любви, но грустно старожилом
Вдруг ощутить себя. Так долго мы живем,
Что, кажется, не кровь идет по жилам,
А неуклюжий чернозем.

Я жив, но я другой, сохранно только имя.
Лишь обернись когда-нибудь -
Там двойники мои верстами соляными
Сопровождают здешний путь.

О если бы я мог, осмелился на йоту
В отвесном громыхании аллей
Вдруг различить связующую ноту
В расстроенном звучанье дней!

1976

To I.B.

There are nights when grass staggers
Under a downpour, when you hear the gutters wheeze.
Roaming in thought, it's easy to wander
Along a monastery's linden alleys.

Every day of my life I feel the asthma
Of Moscow lindens, and long for the dwelling
Where you sullied thick paper with India ink,
And where my past was just beginning.

Haughty girl with your father's easel,
Tell me, was it only yesterday
That the coffeepot whistled till morning
Through kitchens in the Old Arbat?

No, I'm not talking of love, but it's sad to feel
Suddenly like an old fogey. We live so long
It seems no blood moves in the veins,
But lumbering black soil.

I'm alive, but an other, retaining only a name.
Just turn around and look sometime—
My doubles, like pillars of salt,
Follow me on this road.

Oh, if I could've, if I'd dared one bit
In the vertical rumble of linden alleys
In the discord of my days
I might discern now a connecting note.

Сегодня дважды в ночь я видел сон.
Загадочный, по существу, один
И тот же. Так цензура сновидений,
Усердная, щадила мой покой.
На местности условно городской
Столкнулись две машины. Легковую
Тотчас перевернуло. Грузовик
Лишь занесло немного. Лобовое
Стекло его осыпалось на землю,
Осколки же земли не достигали,
И звона не случилось. Тишина
Вообще определяла обстановку.
Покорные реакции цепной,
Автомобили, красные трамваи,
Коверкая железо и людей,
На площадь вылетали, как и прежде,
Но площадь не рассталась с тишиной.
Два битюга (они везли повозку
С молочными бидонами) порвали
Тугую упряжь и скакали прочь.
Меж тем из опрокинутых бидонов
Хлестало молоко, и желоба,
Стальные желоба трамвайных рельсов,
Полны его. Но кровь была черна.
Оцепенев, я сам стоял поодаль
В испарине кошмара. Стихло все.
Вращаться продолжало колесо
Какой-то опрокинутой "Победы".
Спиною к телеграфному столбу
Сидела женщина. Ее черты,
Казалось, были сызмальства знакомы
Душе моей. Но смертная печать
Видна уже была на лике женском.
И тишина.
            Так в клубе деревенском
Киномеханик вечно пьян. Динамик,

✿✿✿

Twice, last night, I dreamt
The same enigmatic dream.
(Thus the diligent censor
Of dreams gave me some peace.)
In what seemed a city, two vehicles
Collided. The car rolled right over.
The truck only skidded a little,
But its glass windshield
Shattered in slivers
Without hitting the ground,
Without making a sound. Silence
Completely defined the scene.
Obeying the chain reaction,
Automobiles, red trolley cars,
Mangling iron and people
Kept flying toward the square,
But the square kept silent.
Two draft horses (dragging a carriage
With sealed milk casks) broke
Their tight harness and galloped away.
Meanwhile, tipped casks
Gushed milk into the gutters,
Filling the steel troughs of trolley rails.
But all the blood was black.
Frozen, I stood at a distance
In the sweat of nightmare. Then all
Grew calm. Only a wheel kept turning
On an overturned car, a Victory.
One woman sat with her back
To a telephone pole. Her features
So familiar, as if my soul had known her
Since infancy. The seal of death
Was already visible on her face.
And silence.
　　　　　　Just as in the village club,
The projectionist's always drunk. The speakers,

Конечно, отказал. И в темноте
Кромешной знай себе стрекочет старый
Проектор. В золотом его луче
Пылинки пляшут. Действие без звука.

Мой тяжкий сон, откуда эта мука?
Мне чудится, что мы у тех времен
Без устали скитаемся на ощупь,
Когда под звук трубы на ту же площадь
Повалим валом с четырех сторон.
Кто скажет заключительное слово
Под сводами последнего Суда,
Когда лиловым сумеркам Брюллова
Настанет срок разлиться навсегда?
Нас смоет с полотняного экрана.
Динамики продует медный вой.
И лопнет высоко над головой
Пифагорейский воздух восьмигранный.

1977

Of course, don't work. And in the inky dark
The old projector chirrs.
Specks of dust are dancing
In the golden light. Action, no sound.

Oh heavy dream, why do we suffer?
These days it seems we wander
Without growing weary. We grope along
Till under the sound of the trumpet
We'll flock together from all directions.
Who'll say the last word
Under the arches of the *Last Day of Pompeii,*
When the time comes for Briullov's lilac dusk
To spill down forever?
We will be washed from the canvas screen.
A brass howl will break through the speakers
And the Pythagorean octagonal air
High above our heads will burst.

✿✿✿

Грешный светлый твой лоб поцелую,
Тотчас хрипло окликну впустую,
Постою, ворочусь домой.
Вот и все. Отключу розетку
Телефона. Запью таблетку
Люминала сырою водой.

Спать пластом поверх одеяла.
Медленно в изголовье встала
Рама, полная звезд одних.
Звезды ходят на цыпочках около
Изголовья, ломятся в стекла -
Только спящему не до них.

Потому что до сумерек надо
Высоту навестить и прохладу
Льда, свободы, воды, камней.
Звук реки - или Терек снежный,
Или кран перекрыт небрежно.
О, как холодно крови моей!

Дальше, главное не отвлекаться.
Засветло предстоит добраться
До шоссе на Владикавказ,
Чтобы утром … Но все по порядку.
Прежде быть на почте. Тридцатку
Получить до закрытия касс.

Чтобы первым экспрессом в Тбилиси
Через нашатырные выси, -
О, как лоб твой светлый горяч!
Авлабар обойду, Окроканы …
Что за чушь! Не закрыты краны -
То ли смех воды, то ли плач -

❖❖❖

I'll kiss your shining sinful forehead,
And hoarsely cry out, in vain,
Then stand around awhile, return home.
That's it. I'll pull the phone
From its socket, and wash down
A phenobarbital with tap water.

To sleep, stretched out, atop the blanket.
Slowly, at the head of the bed,
The window frame rises, full of stars.
Walking on tiptoe near the headboard,
The stars try to break the glass—
But the sleeper has no time for them.

Because a person needs all day
To visit the altitudes and coolness
Of ice, freedom, water, and stones.
Sounds of a river—either snowy Terek
Or the faucet turned off carelessly.
My blood is so cold!

Now then, keep focused.
Before dark, you need to reach
The highway to Vladikavkaz,
So that by morning ... but one thing at a time.
First, get to the post office. Get thirty rubles
Before the closing of the ticket office

So by the first express to Tbilisi
Across ammoniac heights—
O how hot is your bright forehead!
I'll wander Avlabar, Okrokany ...
Damn it. The faucet's not shut—
Whether the water laughs or cries

Не пойму. Не хватало плакать.
Впереди московская слякоть.
На будильнике пятый час.
Ангел мой! Я тебя не неволю.
Для того мне оставлено, что ли,
Море Черное про запас!

1978

I don't know. Tears would be too much.
Ahead, Moscow slush.
The clock says four A.M.
I won't restrain you, my angel.
And why should I, really,
When I have the Black Sea stored away?

❖❖❖

Давным-давно забрели мы на праздник смерти,
Аквариум вещей скорби вовсю прижимая к себе.
Сказочно-страшно стоять в похоронном концерте,
Опрокинутою толпой отразиться в латунной трубе.
В марте шестидесятого за гаражами
Жора вдалбливал нам сексологию и божбу.
Аудитория млела. Внезапно над этажами
Встала на дыбы музыка. Что-то несли в гробу.
Эдаким князем Андреем близ Аустерлица
Поднял я голову в прямоугольное небо двора.
Черные птицы. Три облака. Серые лица.
Выли старухи. Кудахтала детвора.
Детство в марте. Союз воробья и вербы.
Бедное мужество музыки. Старческий гам.
Шапки долой. Очи долу. Лишь небо не знает ущерба.
Старый шарманщик, насилуй осипший орган!

1979

❖❖❖

Long ago, we wandered in on the festival of death,
Pressing up to the aquarium of the things of grief.
It's fairy-tale scary to stand at a burial concert,
Reflected in a brass trumpet as an upside-down crowd.
In March of nineteen sixty behind the garages
Zhora drilled us on sexology and swearing.
The audience thrilled. Suddenly above the floors
Music kicked up. They carried something in a coffin.
Like some Prince Andrei on the battlefield of Austerlitz
I lifted my eyes to the courtyard's rectangle of sky.
Black birds. Three clouds. Gray faces. Old women
Were howling as little kids giggled.
Childhood in March: the union of swallows and willows.
The meager courage of music, the senile din.
Hats off, eyes down. Only the sky knows no sorrow.
Old organ-grinder, coerce the hoarse organ!

❖❖❖

А вот и снег. Есть русские слова
С оскоминой младенческой глюкозы.
Снег валит, тяжелеет голова,
Хоть сырость разводи. Но эти слезы
Иных времен, где в занавеси дрожь,
Бьет соловей, заря плывет по лужам,
Будильник изнемог, и ты встаешь,
Зеленым взрывом тополя разбужен.
Я жил в одной стране. Там тишина
Равно проста в овраге, церкви, поле.
И мне явилась истина одна:
Трудна не боль - однообразье боли.
Я жил в деревне месяц с небольшим.
Прорехи стен латал клоками пакли.
Вслух говорил, слегка переборщил
С риторикой, как в правильном спектакле.

Двустволка опереточной длины,
Часы, кровать, единственная створка
Трюмо, в которой чуть искажены
Кровать с шарами, ходики, двустволка.
Законы жанра - поприще мое.
Меня и в жар бросало, и знобило,
Но драмы злополучное ружье
Висеть висит, но выстрелить забыло.
Мне ждать не внове. Есть здесь кто живой?
Побудь со мной. Поговори со мной.
Сегодня день светлее, чем вчерашний.
Белым-бела вельветовая пашня.
Покурим, незнакомый человек.
Сегодня утром из дому я вышел,
Увидел снег, опешил и услышал
Хорошие слова - а вот и снег.

1978

❖❖❖

Look, it's snowing again. There are words in Russian
That make your mouth burn as if from infant formula.
It snows heavily, the head grows heavy,
You almost feel like crying. But these tears
Are from a different time, where a curtain trembles,
A nightingale wails, dawn swims across puddles ...
The alarm clock exhausted, you finally rise,
Awakened by a green explosion of poplar.
I once lived in the country. There, where silence
Is equally common in ravine, church, or field,
A truth revealed itself to me:
Pain isn't difficult—it's the monotony of pain.
I lived in the village a month or so.
Patched holes in the wall with rags of oakum.
Spoke aloud to myself, my speech
Slightly overdone, like from a proper play.

A double-barrel gun of operettic length,
A clock, a bed, a pier glass, one leaf missing,
The other showing a slightly distorted
Four-poster bed, the wall clock, the gun.
The laws of genre—that's my field.
I was thrown into shivers, fell into fever,
But the ill-starred firearm of the drama
Just hangs there, forgot to fire.
I'm used to waiting. Anyone alive here?
Hang out with me. Come talk to me.
Today's already lighter than yesterday.
The stubble field is whitest white.
Let's have a smoke, stranger.
This morning I left the house and
Glimpsing the snow, was stunned and heard
Those good words—*look, it's snowing again.*

⚜⚜⚜

Здесь реки кричат, как больной под ножом,
Но это сравнение ложь, потому что
Они голосят на стократно чужом
Наречии. Это тебе не Алушта.

Здесь пара волов не тащила арбы
С останками пасмурного Грибоеда.
Суворовско-суриковские орлы
На задницах здесь не справляли победы.

Я шел вверх по Ванчу. Дневная резня
Реки с ледником выдыхалась. Зарница
Цвела чайной розой. Ущелье меня
Встречало недобрым молчаньем зверинца.

Снега пламенели с зарей заодно.
Нагорного неба неграмотный гений
Сам знал себе цену. И было смешно
Сушить эдельвейс в словаре ударений.

Зазнайка-поэзия, спрячем тетрадь:
Есть области мира, живые помимо
Поэзии нашей, - и нам не понять,
Не перевести хриплой речи Памира.

1979

❖❖❖

Here rivers cry like a patient under the knife,
But the comparison fails, because the rivers keen
A dialect one hundred times
More strange. This is no place to vacation.

Here no pair of oxen pulled a cart
With the corpse of gloomy Griboyed.
Here Suvorov's soldiers in Surikov's picture
Didn't slide to victory on their butts.

I went up the Vanch. The day-long carnage
Of river and glacier ran out of steam. Summer
Lightning bloomed like tea rose. The gorge
Met me with the unkind silence of animals caged.

Snow blazed with twilight, in concert.
The illiterate genius of a mountainous sky
Knew its own worth. And it was absurd
To dry edelweiss in a dictionary of dialects.

Conceited poetry, hide the notepad:
There are places in the world beyond
Our words—and we cannot understand,
Can't translate, the Pamir's husky tongue.

матери

Далеко от соленых степей саранчи,
В глухомани, где водятся серые волки,
Вероятно, поныне стоят Баскачи -
Шесть разрозненных изб огородами к Волге.

Лето выдалось скверным на редкость. Дожди
Зарядили. Баркасы на привязи мокли.
Для чего эта малость видна посреди
Прочей памяти, словно сквозь стекла бинокля?

Десять лет погодя я подался в бичи,
Карнавальную накипь оседлых сословий,
И трудился в соленых степях саранчи
У законного финиша волжских верховий.

Для чего мне на грубую память пришло
Пасторальное детство в голубенькой майке?
Сколько, Господи, разной воды утекло
С изначальной поры коммунальной Можайки!

Значит, мы умираем и делу конец.
Просто Волга впадает в Каспийское море.
Всевозможные люди стоят у реки.
Это Волга впадает в Каспийское море.

Все, что с нами случилось, случится опять.
Среди ночи глаза наудачу зажмурю -
Мне исполнится год и тебе двадцать пять.
Фейерверк сизарей растворится в лазури.

Я найду тебя в комнате, зыбкой от слез,
Где стоял КВН, недоносок прогресса,
Где глядела на нас из-под ливня волос
С репродукции старой святая Инесса.

To My Mother

Far past the dusty, locust-filled steppes,
Where gray wolves roam in the wild,
Perhaps Baskachi still exists—
Just six scattered shacks with gardens to the Volga.

That summer was uncommonly foul, raining
Day after day. The boats were drenched
In their slips. Why this, emerging
From the rest of memory, as through a spyglass?

Ten years later, as a migrant laborer,
(Mere clownish scum to the settled class),
I worked in the salty, locust-filled steppes
At the logical conclusion of Volga summits.

Why has a pastoral childhood in blue T-shirt
Come to my hardened memory?
How much water, my God, has flowed by
Since the original age of communal apartments!

It means we're dying, and it's almost all over.
And the Volga runs into the Caspian Sea.
All sorts of people stand on the bank of the river.
This is the Volga flowing to the Caspian Sea.

Everything that's happened to us will happen again.
In the middle of the night I might close my eyes—
I'll be one year old, and you'll be twenty-five.
Fireworks of blue pigeons burst up in azure skies.

I'll find you in an apartment now blurred by tears
Where the first TV stood, preemie of progress,
Where a reproduction of old holy Iness
Would gaze at us from behind a shower of hair.

❖❖❖

Я застану тебя за каким-то шитьем.
Под косящим лучом засверкает иголка.
Помнишь, нам довелось прозябать вчетвером
В деревушке с названьем татарского толка?

КВНовой линзы волшебный кристалл
Синевою нальется. Покажется Волга.
"Ты и впрямь не устала? И я не устал.
Ну, пошли понемногу, отсюда недолго".

1978

❖❖❖

I'll find you mending some clothes.
The needle, under a slanting ray, will gleam.
Remember how cheaply we lived, us four
In this small village with a Tatar name?

The magic crystal of the TV's bulbous eye
Fills up with blue. The Volga appears.
"You're really not tired, Ma? Well, neither am I.
So let's keep going. We're almost there."

Картина мира, милая уму: писатель сочиняет про Муму; шоферы колесят по всей земле со Сталиным на лобовом стекле; любимец телевиденья чабан кастрирует козла во весь экран; агукая, играючи, шутя, мать пестует щекастое дитя. Сдается мне, согражданам не лень усердствовать. В трудах проходит день, а к полночи созреет в аккурат мажорный гимн, как некий виноград.

Бог в помощь всем. Но мой физкультпривет писателю. Писатель (он поэт), несносных наблюдений виртуоз, сквозь окна видит бледный лес берез, вникая в смысл житейских передряг, причуд, коллизий. Вроде бы пустяк по имени хандра, и во врачах нет надобности, но и в мелочах видна утечка жизни. Невзначай он адрес свой забудет или чай на рукопись прольет, то вообще купает галстук бархатный в борще. Смех да и только. Выпал первый снег. На улице какой-то человек, срывая голос, битых два часа отчитывал нашкодившего пса.

Писатель принимается писать. Давно ль он умудрился променять объем на вакуум, проточный звук на паузу? Жизнь валится из рук безделкою, безделицею в щель, внезапно перейдя в разряд вещей еще душемутительных, уже музейных, как-то: баночка драже с истекшим сроком годности, альбом колониальных марок в голубом налете пыли, шелковый шнурок ...

В романе Достоевского "Игрок" описан странный случай. Гувернер влюбился не на шутку, но позор безденежья преследует его. Добро бы лишь его, но существо небесное, предмет любви - и та наделала долгов. О, нищета! Спасая положенье, наш герой сперва, как Германн, вчуже за игрой в рулетку наблюдал, но вот и он выигрывает сдуру миллион. Итак, женитьба? - Дудки! Грозный пыл объемлет бедолагу. Он забыл про барышню, ему предрешено в испарине толкаться в казино. Лишения, долги, потом тюрьма. "Ужели я тогда сошел с ума?" - себя и опечаленных друзей резонно вопрошает Алексей Иванович. А на кого пенять?

Давно ль мы умудрились променять простосердечье, женскую любовь на эти пять похабных рифм: свекровь,

A picture of this world, dear to the mind: a writer composes lines about a mute giant; truckers cross the whole country with Stalin on the front windshield; a television-darling shepherd, looming large on the screen, castrates goats; a mother coos playfully, nurses a chubby-cheeked child. Methinks the citizens never tire in their labors! The day, passing in tasks, will ripen like a cluster of fruit, and exactly at midnight become a major-chord hymn.

God comes to all in need, but this high-five is to the writer. The writer (here a poet), virtuoso of the unbearable observation, sees through windows a pale forest of birch, contemplates the meaning of everyday scrapes, whims, and collisions. It's just a trifle named melancholia: there's no need for a doctor, but life leaks out of everything. He might perchance forget his address or spill tea on a manuscript, or even worse, bathe his velvet tie in borscht. It's so laughable. The first snow has come. On the street someone raises his voice, spends two hours reprimanding his disobedient dog.

The writer gets to writing. How long has it been since he's managed to barter a word for the void, fluid sound for silence? Life, like a trinket, tumbles from his hand into a crevice, suddenly slips into a category of things that still sear the soul, but already are museum-like: a box of chocolates past expiration, an album of colonial stamps in a blue coating of dust, a silk lace.

Dostoyevsky's *The Gambler* describes a strange case. A poor tutor falls madly in love, but the disgrace of his poverty haunts him. It wouldn't be bad if it were just him, but the celestial object of his love has accumulated some debts. O destitution! Our hero saves the day, observing from afar, like Pushkin's Germann, a gambler's tricks. Just like that he wins a million. Beginner's luck. Will he marry? Not a chance. The terrible passion consumes the poor guy. He forgets about the young lady, now doomed to jostle and sweat in the casino. Hardships, debts, then jail. "Was I possessed by some madness then?", Aleksey Ivanovich asks himself and his saddened friends, with good reason. But who else is to blame?

How long have we managed to barter simplicity of heart, a woman's love, for five dark rhymes: brood, blood, head, bread,

кровь, бровь, морковь и вновь! И вновь поэт включает за полночь настольный свет, по комнате описывает круг. Тошнехонько и нужен верный друг. Таким была бы проза. Дай-то Бог. На весь поселок брешет кабыздох. Поэт глядит в холодное окно. Гармония, как это ни смешно, вот цель его, точнее, идеал. Что выиграл он, что он проиграл? Но это разве в картах и лото есть выигрыш и проигрыш. Ни то изящные материи, ни се. Скорее розыгрыш. И это все? Еще не все. Ценить свою беду, найти вверху любимую звезду, испарину труда стереть со лба и сообщить кому-то: "Не судьба".

1982

tread? Treading circles around the room, the poet turns on the desk light past midnight. Life sickens him. He could use a good friend. Prose could be such a friend, God willing. A dog's howl echoes through the whole village. The poet gazes through the cold window. Harmony, however comic it may seem, is his goal. To be precise, his ideal. What has he won, what has he lost? It's only in poker and lotto that someone wins or loses. This is more like a draw. Is that all? No, not all. To value your troubles, to find your favorite star in the sky, to wipe the sweat of work from your brow and say to someone: "it wasn't in the cards."

❖ ❖ ❖

Дай Бог памяти вспомнить работы мои,
Дать отчет обстоятельный в очерке сжатом.
Перво-наперво следует лагерь МЭИ,
Я работал тогда пионерским вожатым.
Там стояли два Ленина: бодрый старик
И угрюмый бутуз серебристого цвета.
По утрам раздавался воинственный крик
“Будь готов”, отражаясь у стен сельсовета.
Было много других серебристых химер -
Знаменосцы, горнисты, скульптура лосихи.
У забора трудился живой пионер,
Утоляя вручную любовь к поварихе.

Жизнерадостный труд мой расцвел колесом
Обозрения с видом от Омска до Оша.
Хватишь лишку и Симонову в унисон
Знай бубнишь помаленьку: “Ты помнишь, Алеша?”
Гадом буду, в столичный театр загляну,
Где примерно полгода за скромную плату
Мы кадили актрисам, роняя слюну,
И катали на фурке тяжелого Плятта.
Верный лозунгу молодости “Будь готов!”,
Я готовился к зрелости неутомимо.
Вот и стал я в неполные тридцать годов
Очарованным странником с пачки “Памира”.

На реке Иртыше говорила резня.
На реке Сырдарье говорили о чуде.
Подвозили, кормили, поили меня
Окаянные ожесточенные люди.
Научился я древней науке вранья,
Разучился спросить о погоде без мата.
Мельтешит предо мной одиссея моя
Кинолентою шосткинского комбината.
Ничего, ничего, ничего не боюсь,
Разве только ленивых убийц в полумасках.

34

❖❖❖

Dear God, let me recall my labors,
To give a detailed account in a concise sketch.
In the beginning there was camp M.E.I.,
Where I worked as a leader of Pioneers.
Two Lenins stood there: cheerful old man
And sullen fat kid of silvery color.
In the mornings the warlike cry "Be prepared"
Reverberated within the walls of the Village Soviet.
There were many other silvery chimeras—
Standard bearers, buglers, a sculpture of an elk.
At the fence a live pioneer toiled hard,
Satisfying by his own hand his love for the cook.

My joyful work blossomed in a merry-
Go-round circling from Omsk to Osh.
Drinking one too many with Simonov,
I muttered to myself: "Remember, Lyosh?"
And I damn near fell into the vaudeville theater,
Where for half a year and meager pay
We slobbered over actresses we served,
And wheeled heavy Platt across the stage.
True to the slogan of my youth—"Be prepared!"
I tirelessly prepared for maturity
So that I became in my stunted thirty years
The enchanted traveler from the pack of "Pamir."

On the Irtish river, daggers spoke loudest.
On the Syrdarya, wonders spoke to us.
God-damned, life-toughened people
Gave me lifts, gave me food and drink.
I learned the ancient science of bullshit.
Always to cuss when asking about weather.
My odyssey passes fast before me
Like a film from the Shostkino factory.
Nothing, nothing, I'm afraid of nothing
Except perhaps the lazy killers in half-masks.

Отшучусь как-нибудь, как-нибудь отсижусь
С Божьей помощью в придурковатых подпасках.

В настоящее время я числюсь при СУ-
206 под началом Н.В.Соткилавы.
Раз в три дня караульную службу несу,
Шельмоватый кавказец содержит ораву
Очарованных странников. Форменный зо-
омузей посетителям на удивленье:
Величанский, Сопровский, Гандлевский, Шаззо -
Часовые строительного управленья.
Разговоры опасные, дождь проливной,
Запрещенные книжки, окурки в жестянке.
Стало быть, продолжается диспут ночной
Чернокнижников Кракова и Саламанки.

Здесь бы мне и осесть, да шалят тормоза.
Ближе к лету уйду, и в минуту ухода
Жизнь моя улыбнется, закроет глаза
И откроет их медленно снова - свобода.
Как впервые, когда рассчитался в МЭИ,
Сдал казенное кладовщику дяде Васе,
Уложил в чемодан причиндалы свои,
Встал ни свет ни заря и пошел восвояси.
Дети спали. Физорг починял силомер.
Повариха дремала в объятьях завхоза.
До свидания, лагерь. Прощай, пионер,
Торопливо глотающий крупные слезы.

1981

Laughing it off with a joke, with God's help
Ducking off among foolish shepherd boys.

At present I'm signed up at the Builder's Corp
Two hundred and six led by Sotkilava.
Once in three days I take the nightwatch.
The cunning Caucasian keeps a whole crew
Of enchanted travelers. Really an authentic zoo-
Logical museum surprising all the visitors—
Velichansky, Soprovsky, Gandlevsky, Shazzo,
The watchguards of the building corporation.
Dangerous conversations, the flooding rain,
Forbidden books, cigarette butts in an empty tin.
Meaning our nightly dispute over blacklisted books
From Krakow and Salamanca continues.

It would be good to stay, but my brakes fail.
Near summer, I'll depart and in the moment of leaving
This life of mine will smile, and close its eyes
And open them slowly again—on freedom.
Like the first time, leaving M.E.I.
I returned the camp rentals to Vasya's storeroom,
Packed my own belongings in a trunk,
Rose before dawn and went into the world.
The children were asleep. Phys. Ed mended the handgrip.
The cook was dozing in the embraces of the Admin.
Good-bye, dear camp. Farewell, Pioneer,
Hurriedly swallowing tears.

❖❖❖

Рабочий, медик ли, прораб ли -
Одним недугом сражены -
Идут простые, словно грабли,
России хмурые сыны.
В ларьке чудовищная баба
Дает "Молдавского" прорабу.
Смиряя свистопляску рук,
Он выпил, скорчился - и вдруг
Над табором советской власти
Легко взмывает и летит,
Печальным демоном глядит
И алчет африканской страсти.
Есть, правда, трезвенники, но
Они, как правило, говно.

Алкоголизм, хоть имя дико,
Но мне ласкает слух оно.
Мы все от мала до велика
Лакали разное вино.
Оно прелестную свободу
Сулит великому народу.
И я, задумчивый поэт,
Прилежно целых девять лет
От одиночества и злости
Искал спасения в вине,
До той поры, когда ко мне
Наведываться стали в гости
Вампиры в рыбьей чешуе
И чертенята на свинье.

Прощай, хранительница дружбы
И саботажница любви!
Благодарю тебя за службу
Да и за пакости твои.
Я ль за тобой не волочился,
Сходился, ссорился, лечился
И вылечился наконец.

❖ ❖ ❖

Struck down with this illness,
The sullen sons of Russia
From doctor to construction super
Shuffle around like lugs.
A monstrous chick in a booth
Gives a bottle to the Super.
Restraining the pandemonium
Of his arm, he drinks, writhes,
And over the gypsy camp of Soviet power
Now soars up with ease, and flies.
He gazes like a sad demon
And craves African passion.
It's true, teetotalers exist
But as a rule they're not worth a shit.

Alcoholism. Though the name is wild,
Just hearing it soothes me.
All us creatures great and small
Lap up different wines.
It promises to a great nation
Delightful freedom.
And I, a pensive poet,
For ten whole years
From loneliness and spite
Searched for salvation
In wine, diligently, until
Vampires in fish scales
And imps riding on swine
Began to visit me.

Farewell, docent of friendship
And saboteur of love!
I thank you for the help,
For the obscenities and tricks.
I chased and caught you,
Fought you, landed in a clinic,
And finally was cured of you.

Веди другого под венец
(Молодоженам честь и место),
Форси в стеклянном пиджаке.
Последний раз к твоей руке
Прильну, стыдливая невеста,
Всплакну и брошу на шарап.
Будь с ней поласковей, прораб.

1979

Lead another couple to the altar,
Ms. Swaggers-in-a-glass-jacket
(All honor and place to the youth).
The last time I kiss
Your hand, bashful bride,
I'll shed a tear, toss you in the air.
Be more gentle with her, Mr. Super.

❖ ❖ ❖

Вот наша улица, допустим,
Орджоникидзержинского,
Родня советским захолустьям,
Но это все-таки Москва.
Вдали топорщатся массивы
Промышленности некрасивой -
Каркасы, трубы, корпуса
Настырно лезут в небеса.
Как видишь, нет примет особых:
Аптека, очередь, фонарь
Под глазом бабы. Всюду гарь.
Рабочие в пунцовых робах
Дорогу много лет подряд
Мостят, ломают, матерят.

Вот автор данного шедевра,
Вдыхая липы и бензин,
Четырнадцать порожних евро-
бутылок тащит в магазин.
Вот женщина немолодая,
Хорошая, почти святая,
Из детской лейки на цветы
Побрызгала и с высоты
Балкона смотрит на дорогу.
На кухне булькает обед,
В квартирах вспыхивает свет.
Ее обманывали много
Родня, любовники, мужья.
Сегодня очередь моя.

Мы здесь росли и превратились
В угрюмых дядь и глупых теть.
Скучали, малость развратились -
Вот наша улица, Господь.
Здесь с окуджававской пластинкой,
Староарбатскою грустинкой
Годами прячут шиш в карман,

❖❖❖

Here's our street, let's say—
Ordzhonikidzerzhinsky.
It could be any Soviet province,
But this is Moscow also.
In the distance the blocks bristle
With the ugliness of heavy industry—
Building skeletons, pipes, complexes
Stubbornly crawl to the heavens.
As you can see, nothing special here—
A drugstore, a line of folks, a shiner
Under a chick's eye. Everywhere, a burning smell.
The workers in orange overalls
Pave, break apart, and curse
The road year after year.

Here's the author of this masterwork
Inhaling linden and gasoline,
Lugging into the store
Fourteen empty bottles for redemption.
And here's the good, no longer young,
Near-saintly woman who splashes water
From a child's watercan on flowers
And looks out on the road
From the balcony's height.
In the kitchen, dinner simmers.
In apartments, lights flare up.
They have let her down often
These kin, these lovers, men.
Today it's my turn.

We grew up here, and now we've changed
Into gloomy uncles and foolish aunts.
We pined away, became a little perverted.
This is our street, dear Lord.
Here with an Okudzhava record
And Old Arbat sentiment,
Year after year, we give the world the finger

43

Испепеляют, как древлян,
Свои дурацкие надежды.
С детьми играют в города -
Чита, Сучан, Караганда.
Ветшают лица и одежды.
Бездельничают рыбаки
У мертвой Яузы-реки.

Такая вот Йокнапатофа
Доигрывает в спортлото
Последний тур (а до потопа
Рукой подать), гадает, кто
Всему виною - Пушкин, что ли?
Мы сдали на пять в этой школе
Науку страха и стыда.
Жизнь кончится - и навсегда
Умолкнут брань и пересуды
Под небом старого двора.
Но знала чертова дыра
Родство сиротства - мы отсюда.
Так по родимому пятну
Детей искали в старину.

1980

Only in our pockets, and burn
Our foolish hopes to ask, like the Drevlan.
With children we play Geography:
Chita, Suchan, Karaganda.
Faces and clothes decay.
The fishermen loiter
At the dead Yauza river.

Such is this Yoknapatawpha:
The last round is ending,
In lotto (the Flood so near
You could touch it). And who's
To blame for all this—Pushkin?
We earned A's in this school
Of the sciences of fear and shame.
Life will end and forever
The swearing and gossip will grow silent
Under the sky of the old yard.
But in this god-forsaken place we knew
A kindred orphanhood. We're from here.
So by a hereditary birthmark
They searched for children in the old days.

❖❖❖

Чикиликанье галок в осеннем дворе
И трезвон перемены в тринадцатой школе.
Росчерк ТУ-104 на чистой заре
И клеймо на скамье "Хабидулин + Оля".
Если б я был не я, а другой человек,
Я бы там вечерами слонялся доныне.
Все в разъезде. Ремонт. Ожидается снег. -
Вот такое кино мне смотреть на чужбине.
Здесь помойные кошки какую-то дрянь
С вожделением делят, такие-сякие.
Вот сейчас он, должно быть, закурит, и впрямь
Не спеша закурил, я курил бы другие.
Хороша наша жизнь - напоит допьяна,
Карамелью снабдит, удивит каруселью,
Шаловлива, глумлива, гневлива, шумна -
Отшумит, не оставив рубля на похмелье …

Если так, перед тем, как уйти под откос,
Пробеги-ка рукой по знакомым октавам,
Наиграй мне по памяти этот наркоз,
Спой дворовую песню с припевом картавым.
Спой, сыграй, расскажи о казенной Москве,
Где пускают метро в половине шестого,
Зачинают детей в госпитальной траве,
Троекратно целуют на Пасху Христову.
Если б я был не я, я бы там произнес
Интересную речь на арене заката.
Вот такое кино мне смотреть на износ
Много лет. Разве это плохая расплата?
Хабидулин выглядывает из окна
Поделиться избыточным опытом, крикнуть -
Спору нет, память мучает, но и она
Умирает - и к этому можно привыкнуть.

1981

❖❖❖

The chatter of daws in the autumn yard,
And the ringing bell in school thirteen.
The signature of a TU-104 plane in clear dawn,
A bench branded "Khabidulin+Olya."
If I were not myself, but another,
I'd hang around there every night. No one's here.
Closed for repairs. Snow's in the forecast.
That's the movie I'd see in a foreign country.
Here in some heaps of trash, junkyard cats
Lustily do it, this way and that. So here this guy
Should, you know, start to smoke, and right away
Does smoke, slowly. I'd smoke a different brand.
Our life is good—it'll get us dead drunk,
Offer us a caramel, amaze us with a carousel,
Rollicking, mocking, furious, noisy—
But it keeps on blaring, no rubles to cure the hangover.

If it's like that, just before going over the edge,
Run your hand over a familiar octave,
Play for me by heart this narcosis,
Sing a backyard song with a guttural refrain.
Sing, play, talk about official Moscow,
Where the metro opens at half past five,
Where kids are conceived on the hospital grass,
And people kiss three times on Easter.
If I weren't myself I'd be the one
Making a memorable speech in the arena of sunset.
I could watch that kind of movie
For many years. Wouldn't be a bad deal.
Khabidulin looks out from the window
To share his excessive experience, and shouts—
No doubt memory is a torment, but even
A memory dies—and you can get used to that.

О.Е.

Ливень лил в Батуми. Лужи были выше
Щиколоток. Стоя под карнизом крыши,
Дух переводили, а до крыши самой
Особняк пиликал оркестровой ямой.
Гаммы, полонезы, польки, баркаролы.
Маленькие классы музыкальной школы.
Черни, Гречанинов, Гедике и Глинка.
Маленькая школа сразу возле рынка.
Скрипка-невеличка, а рояль огромный,
Но еще огромней тот орган загробный.
Глупо огорчаться, это лишь такая
Выдумка, забава, музыка простая.
Звуки пропадали в пресноводном шуме,
Гомоне и плеске. Ливень лил в Батуми.
Выбежали стайкой, по соседству встали
Дети-вундеркинды, лопотали, ждали
Малого просвета. Вскоре посветлело,
И тогда Арчилы, Гиви и Натэлы
Дунули по лужам, улицам, бульварам.
В городе Батуми вровень с тротуаром
Колебалось море, и качался важный
"Адмирал Нахимов" с дом пятиэтажный.
Полно убиваться, есть такое мненье,
Будто эти страсти, грусти, треволненья -
Выдумка, причуда, простенькая полька
Для начальной школы, музыка - и только.

1981

To O.E.

A storm pounded Batumi, puddles deeper
Than ankles. Standing under some eaves,
We caught our breath. From stem to stern
The mansion hummed like an orchestra pit
Scales, polonaises, polkas, and barcaroles.
The elementary grades of a musical school,
The small school right next to the market,
Playing Chorny, Grechaninov, Gedike and Glinka.
The violin was tiny, the piano huge
But the funereal organ biggest of all.
How stupid to get annoyed when it's just
Invention, amusement, simple music.
The sounds were drowned out then by fresh rain,
Commotion and splashes: cloudburst in Batumi.
The wunderkinds ran out in a flock, then stood
Right next to us, murmuring, waiting
For a break in the clouds. Before long, it grew
Light, then all the Archelas, Givis and Natelas
Blew across the puddles, streets, boulevards.
In downtown Batumi the sea was rocking level
With the street, rocking the S.S. Nakhimov,
Pompous cruise ship tall as a five-story house.
Enough mourning. Some are of the opinion
That our terrors, griefs, agitations
Are mere inventions, whims, unpretentious
Grammar-school polkas—music, only music.

❖❖❖

Зверинец коммунальный вымер.
Но в семь утра на кухню в бигуди
Выходит тетя Женя и Владимир
Иванович с русалкой на груди.
Почесывая рыжие подмышки,
Вития замороченной жене
Отцеживает свысока излишки
Премудрости газетной. В стороне
Спросонья чистит мелкую картошку
Океанолог Эрик Ажажа -
Он только из Борнео.

                              Понемножку
Многоголосый гомон этажа
Восходит к поднебесью, чтобы через
Лет двадцать разродиться наконец,
Заполонить мне музыкою череп
И сердце озадачить.

                              Мой отец,
Железом завалив полкоридора,
Мне чинит двухколесный в том углу,
Где тримушки рассеянного Тера
Шуршали всю ангину. На полу -
Ключи, колеса, гайки. Это было,
Поэтому мне мило даже мыло
С налипшим волосом …

                              У нас всего
В избытке: фальши, сплетен, древесины,
Разлуки, канцтоваров. Много хуже
Со счастьем, вроде проще апельсина,
Ан нет его. Есть мненье, что его
Нет вообще, ах, вот оно в чем дело.

Давай живи, смотри не умирай.
Распахнут настежь том прекрасной прозы,
Вовеки не написанной тобой.
Толпою придорожные березы

✿✿✿

The communal zoo has quieted.
But in the kitchen at 7 AM stroll
Vladimir Ivanovich, a mermaid on his chest
And Auntie Zhenya in hair-rollers.
Scratching his red armpits,
The orator filters from on-high
Surpluses of newspaper wisdom
To his gullible wife. Nearby,
The groggy oceanographer
Eric Azhazha peels a small potato.
He just got back from Borneo.
                            Slowly,
The many-voiced din of these rooms
Rises to the edge of heaven, so that in
Twenty years it finally bears
Fruit, filling my skull with music,
Perplexing my heart.
                            My father,
Blocking half the hallway with iron,
Repairs my two-wheeler in that corner,
Where *Three Musky Tears*
Rustled in my fever. On the floor—
Keys, wheels, nuts. So much happened here
Even the soap stuck with hair
Is dear to me ...
                            We had plenty
Of hypocrisy, gossip, partings, stolen
Boards and office supplies. We had less
Happiness, as if it were simple as an orange.
Really, there wasn't any. Some folks believe
It doesn't exist at all—not that it matters.

Keep living, then, don't even think of dying.
The volume of great prose is flung open,
Forever not written by you.
The birches lining the roadside run

Бегут и опрокинутой толпой
Стремглав уходят в зеркало вагона.

С утра в ушах стоит галдеж ворон.
С локомотивом мокрая ворона
Тягается, и головной вагон
Теряется в неведомых пределах.
Дожить до оглавления, до белых
Мух осени. В начале букваря
Отец бежит вдоль изгороди сада
Вслед за велосипедом, чтобы чадо
Не сверзилось на гравий пустыря.

Сдается мне, я старюсь. Попугаев
И без меня хватает. Стыдно мне
Мусолить малолетство, пусть Катаев,
Засахаренный в старческой слюне,
Сюсюкает. Дались мне эти черти
С ободранных обоев или слизни
На дачном частоколе, но гудит
Там, за спиной, такая пропасть смерти,
Которая посередине жизни
Уже в глаза внимательно глядит.

1981

As if in a crowd, and like a rushing crowd
Fall headlong in the mirror on the train.

Since dawn, the squawks of crows ringing your ears.
A glistening crow outcries the locomotive, the engine
Disappearing into parts unknown.
To live until the afterword, till the white fly
Of autumn flutters down. On the primer's first page
Father runs along the orchard fence
Behind the bicycle, keeping his child
From tumbling to the gravel of a vacant lot.

I think I'm getting old. There are enough
Parrots without me. I'm ashamed
Of wearing my younger years thin—let Kataev,
Candied in senile saliva, do the lisping.
I couldn't care less about these devils
Of ragged wallpaper or the slugs
On the dacha palisade, but behind
An abyss of death drones,
That in the middle of life already
Gazes at me, attentively, in the eyes.

❖❖❖

Светало поздно. Одеяло
Сползало на пол. Сизый свет
Сквозь жалюзи мало-помалу
Скользил с предмета на предмет.
По мере шаткого скольженья,
Раздваивая светотень,
Луч бил наискосок в "Оленью
Охоту". Трепетный олень
Летел стремглав. Охотник пылкий
Облокотился на приклад.
Свет трогал тусклые бутылки
И лиловатый виноград
Вчерашней трапезы, колоду
Игральных карт и кожуру
Граната, в зеркале комода
Чертил зигзаги. По двору
Плыл пьяный запах - гнали чачу.
Индюк барахтался в пыли.
Пошли слоняться наудачу,
Куда глаза глядят пошли.
Вскарабкайся на холм соседний,
Увидишь с этой высоты,
Что ночью первый снег осенний
Одел далекие хребты.
На пасмурном булыжном пляже
Откроешь пачку сигарет.
Есть в этом мусорном пейзаже
Какой-то тягостный секрет.
Газета, сломанные грабли,
Заржавленные якоря.
Позеленели и озябли
Косые волны октября.
Наверняка по краю шири
Вдоль горизонта серых вод
Пройдет без четверти четыре
Экскурсионный теплоход
"Сухум-Батум" с заходом в Поти.

❖❖❖

Twilight came late. The blanket
Slipped to the floor. A gray light
Poked through blinds, glided
Around, from object to object.
In an unsteady composition
Dividing dark from shadow
The light struck obliquely on
"The Hunt." An anxious doe
Flying headlong, an ardent hunter
Leaning elbows on a rifle butt.
One ray touched tarnished bottles
And grapes the color of violets
From last night's feast, a deck
Of cards, pomegranate rind,
And in the dresser's mirror
Drew zigzags. Across the yard
Drifted a drunken smell, distilled.
A turkey wallowed in the dust.
We went then, and loitered aimless.
We went wherever feet took us.
Clamber up a neighboring hill,
You'll see from this height
The very first snow of fall
Draped the distant ridge overnight.
On a bleak and cobbled beach
You'll open a pack of cigarettes.
In this trash-filled landscape
There's some painful secret.
Newspapers, broken rakes,
Anchors crusted with rust.
The slanting October waves
Looked greenish and cold.
Over there, no doubt,
On the horizon of gray water
A sightseeing cruise boat
Will go by at a quarter to four,
The Sukhumi-Batumi via Poti.

Он служит много лет подряд,
И чайки в бреющем полете
Над ним горланят и парят.
Я плавал этим теплоходом.
Он переполнен, даже трюм
Битком набит курортным сбродом -
Попойка, сутолока, шум.
Там нарасхват плохое пиво,
Диск "Бони М", духи "Кармен".
На верхней палубе лениво
Господствует нацмен-бармен.
Он "чита-брита" напевает,
Глаза блудливые косит,
Он наливает, как играет,
Над головой его висит
Генералиссимус, а рядом
В овальной рамке из фольги,
Синея вышколенным взглядом,
С немецкой розовой ноги
Красавица капрон спускает.
Поют и пьют на все лады,
А за винтом, шипя, сверкает
Живая изморозь воды.
Сойди с двенадцати ступенек
За багажом в похмельный трюм.
Печали много, мало денег -
В иллюминаторе Батум.
На пристани, дыша сивухой,
Поможет в поисках жилья
Железнозубая старуха -
Такою будет смерть моя …
Давай вставай, пошли без цели
Сквозь ежевику пустыря.
Озябли и позеленели
Косые волны октября.
Включали свет, темнело рано.
Мой незадачливый стрелок
Дремал над спинкою дивана,

It has for many years in a row.
Seagulls in circling flight
Above the boat hover and cry.
I've taken that cruise before.
It's always crowded, even below,
Stuffed with tourist morons,
Drinking bouts, din, commotion.
Bad beer's always in demand,
Boney M, stink of "Carmen."
And the lazy local barman
Who rules the upper floors
Sings all the pop hits,
Squints his lascivious eyes,
Pours, sometimes plays.
Over his head hangs
Generalissimo. Nearby,
In an oval foil frame,
Visible to the trained eye,
A rosy-legged beauty
Bares her German panties.
Song and drink in every corner.
Behind the boat, hissing, seethes
A living frosted water.
Walk down twelve stairs
To a drunken hold for baggage.
There's little money, much despair—
In the porthole: Batumi emerges.
On the pier, an old crone waits,
Breathing raw vodka, iron-toothed
And helpful in searches for roofs.
Thus will be my angel of death.
We went up then, without any goal
Through blackberry wastelands.
The slanting October waves
Looked greenish and cold.
Houses lit, sun already set.
And my luckless arrow slept
Above the back of a sofa—

Олень летел, не чуя ног.
Вот так и жить. Тянуть боржоми.
Махнуть рукой на календарь.
Все в участи приемлю, кроме …
Но это, как писали встарь,
Предмет особого рассказа,
Мне снится тихое село
Неподалеку от Кавказа.
Доселе в памяти светло.

1980

A deer flew, not feeling its legs.
This is the life. Swig some seltzer,
Shrug off the calendar.
I accept my entire fate, except ...
But that, as the ancients say,
Is a story for another day.
I dream of a quiet hamlet
Not far from the Caucasus.
For now, my memory's light.

❖❖❖

В начале декабря, когда природе снится
Осенний ледоход, кунсткамера зимы,
Мне в голову пришло немного полечиться
В больнице #3, что около тюрьмы.
Больные всех сортов - нас было девяносто, -
Канканом вещих снов изрядно смущены,
Бродили парами в пижамах не по росту
Овальным двориком Матросской Тишины.

И день-деньской этаж толкался, точно рынок.
Подъем, прогулка, сон, мытье полов, отбой.
Я помню тихий холл, аквариум без рыбок -
Сор памяти моей не вымести метлой.
Больничный ветеран учил меня, невежду,
Железкой отворять запоры изнутри.
С тех пор я уходил в бега, добыв одежду,
Но возвращался спать в больницу #3.

Вот повод для стихов с туманной подоплекой.
О жизни взаперти, шлифующей ключи
От собственной тюрьмы. О жизни, одинокой
Вне собственной тюрьмы ... Учитель, не учи.
Бог с этой мудростью, мой призрачный читатель!
Скорбь тайную мою вовеки не сведу
За здорово живешь под общий знаменатель
Игривый общих мест. Я прыгал на ходу

В трамвай. Шел мокрый снег. Сограждане качали
Трамвайные права. Вверху на все лады
Невидимый тапер на дедовском рояле
Озвучивал кино надежды и нужды.
Так что же: звукоряд, который еле слышу,
Традиционный бред поэтов и калек
Или аттракцион - бегут ручные мыши
В игрушечный вагон - и валит серый снег?

❖❖❖

In the beginning of December, when nature dreams
Of autumn ice-drifts, of winter's cabinet of curiosities,
I got it in my head to undergo treatment
At Psych Hospital #3, the one next to the jail.
Maimed patients of all sorts—ninety of us total—
Troubled with the can-can of prophetic dreams
Rambled in pairs in our ill-fitting pajamas
Around the oval yard of Sailor's Silence.

All day long the floor jostled like a market.
Reveille, saunter, sleep, clean floors, retreat.
I remember a quiet hall, an aquarium without fish—
A broom won't sweep away the litter of memory.
A hospital veteran taught me, an ignoramus,
To pick a lock from the inside with a piece of iron.
After that I made my getaway, procured street clothes,
But returned to sleep in Hospital #3.

Here's occasion for a poem with a dark motive.
About life locked up, grinding a perfect key
From one's own jail. Or about a lonely life
Outside one's own jail ... Teacher, spare us the lecture.
To hell with such profundity, my spectral reader!
I would never bring my secret grief and life
Under the playful common denominator
For nothing. On the run I jumped

The trolley. A wet snow fell. Fellow citizens swayed
To the trolley's rules. Above, in every key
An invisible ballroom pianist at a grand piano
Scored out the film of hope and dire need.
Is this musical scale I hardly hear
The traditional delirium of poets and cripples
Or a carnival attraction (the tamed mice running
In a toy car) with gray snow heavily falling?

Печальный был декабрь. Куда я ни стучался
С предчувствием моим, мне верили с трудом.
Да будет ли конец - роптала кровь. Кончался
Мой бедный карнавал. Пора и в желтый дом.
Когда я засыпал, больничная палата
Впускала снегопад, оцепенелый лес,
Вокзал в провинции, окружность циферблата -
Смеркается. Мне ждать, а времени в обрез.

1982

That December was sad. No matter where I knocked
To share my premonitions, they barely believed me.
Will this ever end?—the blood grumbled.
My small carnival's over. Time for the madhouse.
When I'd fall asleep, the hospital room
Let in snowfall, the torpid forest,
A train station deep in the country, the clock face—
Twilight. I have to wait, but have no time to spare.

❖ ❖ ❖

Самосуд неожиданной зрелости,
Это зрелище средней руки
Лишено общепризнанной прелести -
Выйти на берег тихой реки,
Рефлектируя в рифму. Молчание
Речь мою караулит давно.
Бархударов, Крючков и компания,
Разве это нам свыше дано!

Есть обычай у русской поэзии
С отвращением бить зеркала
Или прятать кухонное лезвие
В ящик письменного стола.
Дядя в шляпе, испачканной голубем,
Отразился в трофейном трюмо.
Не мори меня творческим голодом,
Так оно получилось само.

Было вроде кораблика, ялика,
Воробья на пустом гамаке.
Это облако? Нет, это яблоко.
Это азбука в женской руке.
Это азбучной нежности навыки,
Скрип уключин по дачным прудам.
Лижет ссадину, просится на руки -
Я тебя никому не отдам!

Стало барщиной, ревностью, мукою,
Расплескался по капле мотив.
Всухомятку мычу и мяукаю,
Пятернями башку обхватив.
Для чего мне досталась в наследие
Чья-то маска с двусмысленным ртом,
Одноактовой жизни трагедия,
Диалог резонера с шутом?

The lynch law of sudden maturity:
This mediocre spectacle
Lacks the general pleasure
Of walking the shore of a quiet river,
Reflecting in rhyme. Silence
Too long has guarded my words.
The great grammarians
Seem like gifts from the gods!

There is a custom in Russian poetry
Of breaking mirrors with disgust
Or concealing kitchen knives
In the drawers of writing desks.
A guy in a hat spattered by a pigeon
Reflected in a pier-glass captured in the War.
Don't starve me with creative hunger—
That's come quite on its own power.

It was like a ship, a yawl,
Sparrows in an empty hammock.
Is it a cloud? No, it's an apple,
An alphabet in a woman's hand.
The alphabet of tender habits,
Scrape of oarlocks on dacha ponds.
She licks a scab, asks to be held—
I won't give you up to anyone.

Slavery, jealousy, and torture,
Themes spilling drop by drop—
I moo, mew, eat dry crusts without water,
Holding my head in my palms.
Why must I have as my inheritance
A mask with an ambiguous mouth,
The tragedy of a one-act life,
A preacher's dialogue with a fool?

Для чего, моя музыка зыбкая,
Объясни мне, когда я умру,
Ты сидела с недоброй улыбкою
На одном бесконечном пиру
И морочила сонного отрока,
Скатерть праздничную теребя?
Это яблоко? Нет, это облако.
И пощады не жду от тебя.

1982

My unsteady music,
Explain to me when I die,
Why you sat with an unkind smile
At an unendless feast
And fooled the dreamy child
Who plucked at a holiday tablecloth?
Is it an apple? No, it's a cloud.
I don't expect you to have mercy.

Д.Пригову

Отечество, предание, геройство ...
Бывало, раньше мчится скорый поезд -
Пути разобраны по недосмотру.
Похоже, катастрофа неизбежна,
А там ведь люди. Входит пионер,
Ступает на участок аварийный,
Снимает красный галстук с тонкой шеи
И яркой тканью машет. Машинист
Выглядывает из локомотива
И понимает: что-то здесь не так.
Умело рычаги перебирает -
И катастрофа предупреждена.

Или другой пример. Несется скорый.
Пути разобраны по недосмотру.
Похоже, катастрофа неизбежна.
А там ведь люди. Стрелочник-старик
Выходит на участок аварийный,
Складным ножом себе вскрывает вены,
Горячей кровью тряпку обагряет
И яркой тканью машет. Машинист
Выглядывает из локомотива
И понимает: что-то здесь не так.
Умело рычаги перебирает -
И катастрофа предупреждена.

А в наше время, если едет поезд,
Исправный путь лежит до горизонта.
Условия на диво, знай, учись
Или работай, или совмещай
Работу с обучением заочным.
Все изменилось. Вырос пионер.
Слегка обрюзг, вполне остепенился,
Начальником стал железнодорожным,
На стрелочника старого орет,
Грозится в ЛТП его упрятать.

1983

To Dmitry Prigov

Fatherland, and tradition, and heroism …
It used to happen the express sped forward—
The tracks were dismantled, an oversight.
A catastrophe seemed unavoidable,
And with people there! A Pioneer came by,
Stepped to the place of the breakdown,
Took the red tie from his thin neck
And waved the bright cloth. The engineer
Looked out from the locomotive
And understood something wasn't right.
He quickly pulled all the levers—
And thus a catastrophe was averted.

Or, another example. The express rushed along.
The tracks were dismantled, an oversight.
A catastrophe seemed unavoidable,
And with people there! An old switchman
Stepped to the place of the breakdown,
And with a pocket knife cut open a vein,
Stained the rag with seething blood
And waved the bright cloth. The engineer
Looked out from the locomotive
And understood something wasn't right.
He quickly pulled all the levers—
And thus a catastrophe was averted.

But today, if the train still runs,
The straight track stretches to the horizon.
The time is right, you know,
To study or work, or combine
Work with a correspondence course.
Everything's changed. The Pioneer's grown,
Turned chubby, sown his wild oats
And become the chief of the railroad,
Bawling out the old switchman,
Threatening to send him to rehab.

69

ЭЛЕГИЯ

Мне холодно. Прозрачная весна ...
О.Мандельштам

Апреля цирковая музыка -
Трамваи, саксофон, вороны -
Накроет кладбище Миусское
Запанибрата с похоронной.
Был или нет я здесь по случаю,
Рифмуя на живую нитку?
И вот доселе сердце мучаю,
Все пригодилось недобитку.
И разом вспомнишь, как там дышится,
Какая слышится там гамма.
И синий с предисловьем Дымшица
Выходит томик Мандельштама.
Как раз и молодость кончается,
Гербарный василек в тетради.
Кто в США, кто в Коми мается,
Как некогда сказал Саади.
А ты живешь свою подробную,
Теряешь совесть, ждешь трамвая
И речи слушаешь надгробные,
Шарф подбородком уминая.
Когда задаром - тем и дорого -
С экзальтированным протестом
Трубит саксофонист из города
Неаполя. Видать, проездом.

1985

Elegy

I'm cold. Transparent spring . . .
—Osip Mandelstam

The circus music of April—
Trolleys, saxophone, crows—
Covers Miussky cemetery,
Invites itself to a funeral.
Did you come by chance alone,
Rhyming any way you can?
Till now your heart was a torment,
But you'll take anything when desperate.
Then you'll remember the cool air,
How you heard music around you.
How the first Mandelstam book came out:
Slim, dark blue, prefaced by Dymschitz.
And just like that youth ended,
A fragrant cornflower in a notebook.
Who's in the U.S., who's suffering in Komi,
As the poet Sadi said long ago.
And you live your minute details,
Lose your honor, wait for the trolley
And listen to graveside orations,
Chin crumpled down on your scarf.
Free of charge—all the more dear—
The saxophonist from Naples blows
His exalted protesting blues.
Must be passing through.

Б.Кенжееву

Мое почтение. Есть в пасмурной отчизне
Таможенный обряд, и он тебе знаком:
Как будто гасят свет - и человек при жизни
Уходит в темноту лицом и пиджаком.

Кенжеев, не хандри. Тебя-то неуместно
Учить тому-сему или стращать Кремлем.
Терпи. В Америке, насколько мне известно,
Свобода, и овцу рифмуют с кораблем.

Я сам не весельчак. Намедни нанял дачу,
Уже двухкомнатную, вскладчину с попом.
Артачусь с пьяных глаз, с похмелья горько плачу,
Откладывая жить на вечное потом.

Чего б вам пожелать реального? Во-первых,
Здоровья. Вылезай из насморков своих,
Питайся трижды в день, не забывай о нервах
Красавицы-жены, пей в меру. Во-вторых,

Расти детеныша, не бей ремнем до срока,
Сноси безропотно пеленки, нищету,
Пренебрежение. Купи брошюру Спока,
Читай ее себе, Лауре и коту.

За окнами октябрь. Вокруг приметы быта:
Будильник, шифоньер, в кастрюле пять яиц.
На письменном столе лежит "Бхагаватгита" -
За месяц я прочел четырнадцать страниц.

Там есть один мотив: сердечная тревога
Боится творчества и ладит с суетой.
Для счастья нужен мир, казалось бы, немного.
Но, если мира нет, то счастье - звук пустой.

To Bakhyt Kenjeev

My regards. There is in the sullen homeland
A ritual at the border—you remember it:
As if a light were turned off, a living person
Goes out in the dark, just a face and jacket.

Kenjeev, don't despair. I know it's not my place
To teach you anything or to scare you with the Kremlin.
Endure. In America, as far as I know,
Freedom exists, and "sheep" rhymes with "ship."

I'm also hardly the life of the party. I just rented a dacha
With two rooms, pooled money with a priest.
I'm stubborn when drunk, weep when hung over,
Put off living for some eternal later.

What do I really wish for you? Well, first,
Think of your health. Climb out of your colds,
Eat three squares a day, don't forget the worries
Of a beautiful wife, drink in moderation. Second,

Raise your young cub, don't belt him too early.
Bear without complaint the diapers, poverty,
And neglect. Buy a book by Dr. Spock,
Read it to yourself, Laura, and the cat.

Beyond windows, October. Around, signs of life:
Alarm clock, chest of drawers, five eggs
In a pot. On the table, *The Bhaghavad-Gita*—
In a month I've read fourteen pages.

There, the single theme: a heart in its unease
Fears creativity and becomes a friend of vanity.
You only need a little peace to be happy.
But without any peace, happiness is empty.

Поэтому твори. Немало причинила
Жизнь всякого, да мы и сами хороши.
Но были же любовь и бледные чернила
Карельской заводи … Пожалуйста, пиши

С оказией и без. Целуй семейство пылко.
Быть может, в будущем - далеко-далеко
Сойдемся запросто, откупорим бутылку -
Два старых болтуна, но дышится легко.

1982

Therefore, create. Life has caused us
Not a little trouble, though we've done our part.
But love and the pale ink of a Karelia lake
Did exist … So please, write

If you get the chance, or not. Kiss the family.
And perhaps, somewhere far, far in the future,
We'll get together, uncork a bottle without fanfare—
Two old blowhards, yes, but breathing easy.

❀ ❀ ❀

Ай да сирень в этом мае! Выпуклокрупные гроздья
Валят плетни в деревнях, а на Бульварном кольце
Тронут лицо в темноте - душемутительный запах.
Сердце рукою сдави, восвояси иди, как слепой.
Здесь на бульварах впервой повстречался мне
                                    голый дошкольник,
Лучник с лукавым лицом; изрядно стреляет малец!
Много воды утекло. Старая только заноза
В мякоти чудом цела. Думаю, это пройдет.
Поутру здесь я сидел нога на ногу гордо у входа
В мрачную пропасть метро с ветвью сирени в руках.
Кольца пускал из ноздрей, пил в час пик газировку,
Улыбнулся и рек согражданам в сердце своем:
"Дурни, куда вы толпой? Олухи, мне девятнадцать.
Сроду нигде не служил, не собираюсь и впредь.
Знаете тайну мою? Моей вы не знаете тайны:
Ночь я провел у Лаисы. Виктор Зоилыч рогат".

1984

❁ ❁ ❁

Oh, the lilacs this May! Bulging bunches fell
Fences in the villages, and on the ring of boulevards
They touch your face in the darkness—a smell to stir the soul.
Squeeze your heart in your hand; go home like a blind man.
I first met that naked kindergartner here on the boulevard—
An archer with a sly look. And I must say, that kid can shoot!
Much water's passed under the bridge. Only an old splinter
In the flesh is miraculously intact. I think it'll pass.
But that morning, I sat here cross-legged and proud at the entrance
To a gloomy cave of the metro, lilac branch in hand.
I sent a smoke-ring from my nostril, drank soda in rush hour,
Smiled and spoke in my heart to my fellow citizens:
"Fools, where are you heading, all in a crowd? Dolts, I'm 19.
I've never held down a job, not planning to anytime soon.
But do you know my secret? Can't you guess my secret?
I spent last night at Laisa's—Victor Zoilich is now a cuckold."

❖ ❖ ❖

Устроиться на автобазу
И петь про черный пистолет.
К старухе матери ни разу
Не заглянуть за десять лет.
Проездом из Газлей на юге
С канистры кислого вина
Одной подруге из Калуги
Заделать сдуру пацана.
В рыгаловке рагу по средам,
Горох с треской по четвергам.
Божиться другу за обедом
Впаять завгару по рогам.
Преодолеть попутный гребень
Тридцатилетия. Чем свет,
Возить "налево" лес и щебень
И петь про черный пистолет.
А не обломится халтура -
Уснуть щекою на руле,
Спросонья вспоминая хмуро
Махаловку в Махачкале.

1985

❖❖❖

To land a job at the garage
And sing about a black pistol.
And not once in ten years
Stop and visit your old mother.
En route from Gazli in the south
After a canister of sour wine
Screw some girlfriend from Kaluga,
Leave her when she's pregnant.
Gaseteria lamb on Wednesdays,
Cod-pea soup on Thursdays.
To vow to a friend at lunch
To rough up a garage owner, then
Surmount the promising crest
Of a thirtieth birthday. At dawn
To drive for black market gravel
And sing the black pistol.
And if not lucky enough for this,
To drift off—cheek on the steering wheel—
To sleep, remembering gloomily
A brawl in the Caucasus.

А. *Магарику*

Что-нибудь о тюрьме и разлуке,
Со слезою и пеной у рта.
Кострома ли, Великие Луки -
Но в застолье в чести Воркута.
Это песни о том, как по справке
Сын седым воротился домой.
Пил у Нинки и плакал у Клавки -
Ах ты, Господи Боже ты мой!

Наша станция, как на ладони.
Шепелявит свое водосток.
О разлуке поют на перроне.
Хулиганов везут на восток.
День-деньской колесят по отчизне
Люди, хлеб, стратегический груз.
Что-нибудь о загубленной жизни -
У меня невзыскательный вкус.

Выйди осенью в чистое поле,
Ветром родины лоб остуди.
Жаркой розой глоток алкоголя
Разворачивается в груди.
Кружит ночь из семейства вороньих.
Расстояния свищут в кулак.
Для отечества нет посторонних,
Нет, и все тут - и дышится так,

Будто пасмурным утром проснулся
Загремели, баланду внесли, -
От дурацких надежд отмахнулся,
И в исподнем ведут, а вдали -
Пруд, покрытый гусиною кожей,
Семафор через силу горит,
Сеет дождь, и небритый прохожий
Сам с собой на ходу говорит.

1984

To Aleksey Magarik

Sing something about prison and parting,
With tears and a mouth full of foam.
Something from Kostroma or Velikie Luki
But when drinking, something about the gulag.
This song's about how a son finally came home
On medical leave, his hair gone white.
He drank at Ninka's, cried at Klavka's—
My God, my God, have you forgiven us?

Our train station, visible for miles around:
A gutter lisping to itself,
Someone singing of platform farewells,
Of hooligans taken to the east.
Of people, bread, strategic cargo
Traveling the homeland all day.
A song about wasted life—
I'm not particular, just play.

In the fall, go out to the open fields,
Cool your head in homeland wind.
A swallow of alcohol is like a hot rose,
Unfolding in your chest.
The night of the ravens hovers above.
Distances whistle through fingers.
The homeland has no strangers,
No, everything's here, and you breathe as if

You woke to an overcast dawn ...
The door clangs, the gruel's brought in,
You brush off your foolish hopes—
And are taken in your underwear. In the distance,
A pond is covered in gooseflesh,
A semaphore forces itself to shine,
Rain scatters down, and an unshaven man
Talks to himself as he passes by.

П.Мовчану

Поездка: автобус, безбожно кренясь,
Пылит большаком, не езда, а мученье.
Откуда? куда он? на Верхнюю Грязь?
Из Лога? в Кресты? - не имеет значенья.
Попутчики: дядя с двуручной пилой,
Две тетки, подросток с улыбкой острожной,
Изрядно поддавши мужик пожилой
И в меру поддавши рабочий дорожный.
Кто спит, кто с похмелья, кто навеселе.
В проеме окна поднебесное поле.
Здесь все - вплоть до Гундаревой на стекле -
Смесь яви и сна и знакомо до боли.
Встречь ветру прохожая тащит ведро
Брусники и всякую всячину в торбе.
Есть сходство с известной картиной Коро,
Но больше знакомых деталей и скорби.
Все это, родное само по себе,
Тем втрое родней, что озвучено соло
На третьей, обещанной грозной трубе,
Той самой. И снова деревни и села.
И надо б, как сказано, в горы бежать,
Коль скоро вода от полыни прогоркла.
Но наша округа - бескрайняя гладь,
На сутки пути ни холма, ни пригорка.

1987

To Pavel Movchan (Outside Chernobyl)

A journey. The bus careens shamelessly,
Blows up a cloud of dust—not a ride, but a torture.
Where is it going, Muddy Valley? Kresti?
Where is it from, Ravine? It doesn't matter.
My fellow travelers, a guy with a two-handled saw,
Two babushkas, a teen with a criminal smile,
An old muzhik quite well oiled
And a construction worker pretty drunk himself—
Everyone sleeping, hungover, or trashed.
In the window, a field yielding to sky. It's all here,
Right to the starlet on the windshield—
Both dream and real, and painfully familiar.
A passerby, leaning into wind, carries a bucket
Of berries and a bulging burlap sack.
Just like that painting by Corot,
But with more familiar details, more sorrow.
All this, native and dear in itself,
I love three times more, now that the musical score
Calls for the menacing third trumpet.
The prophesied final solo. Outside, town after town.
We should, as it's written, head for the mountains
When water grows bitter from wormwood.
But this place is a boundless plain,
Not a hill or knoll a day in any direction.

Е.Ф.Фадеевой

Не сменить ли пластинку? Но родина снится опять.
Отираясь от нечего делать в вокзальном народе,
Жду своей электрички, поскольку намерен сажать
То ли яблоню, то ли крыжовник. Сентябрь на исходе.
Снится мне, что мне снится, как еду по длинной стране
Приспособить какую-то важную доску к сараю.
Перспектива из снов - сон во сне, сон во сне, сон во сне.
И курю в огороде на корточках, время теряю.
И по скверной дороге иду восвояси с шести
Узаконенных соток на жалобный крик электрички.
Вот ведь спички забыл, а вернешься - не будет пути,
И стучусь наобум, чтобы вынесли - как его - спички.
И чужая старуха выходит на низкий порог,
И моргает, и шамкает, будто она виновата,
Что в округе ненастье и нету проезжих дорог,
А в субботу в Покровском у клуба сцепились ребята,
В том, что я ошиваюсь на свете дурак дураком
На осеннем ветру с незажженной своей сигаретой,
Будто только она виновата и в том, и в другом,
И во всем остальном, и в несчастиях родины этой.

1987

To E.F. Fadeeva

It's time to change the record—but I'm dreaming again
Of the motherland. Bored, shouldering past crowds
At the station, I wait for the train, since I intend to grow
Some apples or gooseberries. September's leaving.
I dream that I'm just dreaming of crossing a wide country
To nail some important scrap of board to a shed.
Perspective of dreams is a dream within a dream within a dream.
I smoke, squat down in a potato patch, burn off time.
And over the muddy road I head home,
From my small dacha plots toward the train's plaintive cry.
But damn, no matches, and it's bad luck to go back.
So I knock at random doors along the way. Matches.
And a strange old woman leans through a low frame
And blinks and mumbles as if she were to blame
That the weather's bad and there are no smooth roads
That on Saturday at the club the guys came to blows
That I wander this world like a fool,
An unlit cigarette in a mid-autumn gale—
As if she were to blame for this and that,
And for the rest, for the troubles of the motherland.

❖❖❖

Косых Семен. В запое с Первомая.
Сегодня вторник. Он глядит в окно,
Дрожит и щурится, не понимая
Еще темно или уже темно.
Я знаю умонастроенье это
И сам, кружа по комнате тоски,
Цитирую кого-то: "Больше света",
Со злостью наступая на шнурки.
Когда я первые стихотворенья,
Волнуясь, сочинял свои
И от волнения и неуменья
Все строчки начинал с союза "и",
Мне не хватило кликов лебединых,
Ребячливости, пороха, огня,
И тетя Муза в крашеных сединах
Сверкнула фиксой, глядя на меня.
И ахнул я: бывают же ошибки!
Влюблен бездельник, но в кого влюблен!
Концерт для струнных, чембало и скрипки,
Увы, не воспоследует, Семен.
И встречный ангел, шедший пустырями,
Отверз мне, варвару, уста,
И - высказался я. Но тем упрямей
Склоняют своенравные лета
К поруганной игре воображенья,
К завещанной насмешке над толпой,
К поэзии, прости за выраженье,
Прочь от суровой прозы.

                      Но, тупой,
От опыта паду до анекдота.
Ну, скажем так: окончена работа.
Супруг супруге накупил обнов,
Врывается в квартиру, смотрит в оба,
Распахивает дверцы гардероба,
А там - Никулин, Вицин, Моргунов.

1990

❖❖❖

Semyon Kosikh, drunk since May Day.
Now it's Tuesday. He looks out the window,
Trembles and squints, uncertain
If it's still dark, or already dark.
I've known his frame of mind well.
Circling that melancholy room,
I quote some guy—"more light"—
And trip over my laces in a fury.
When I first began to write,
Exhilaration, agitation
And clumsy skill made all my lines
Begin with the breathless "and."
And I soon ran out of swan's cries,
Childishness, gunpowder, and fire.
In dyed gray hair, Auntie Muse
Flashed her foil tooth, gazed at me.
And I exclaimed, "Accidents happen!
This bum's in love, but with you?"
A concert for strings, chembalo, violin,
Alas, won't follow, Semyon.
Having braved wastelands, the angel
Approached, opened my barbarian mouth,
And—that's all I can say. But all the more
Stubbornly do the headstrong years bend me
To the profaned game of imagination,
To the testamentary sneer above the crowd,
To poetry (pardon the expression),
To hell with desiccated prose.
                              But dulled
By experience, I'll resort to a joke.
Something like this: his work done,
A husband buys his wife some dresses,
Bursts into the room, glances about,
Throws the wardrobe doors open.
Harpo, Chico, and Groucho all fall out.

❖❖❖

Вот когда человек средних лет, багровея, шнурки
Наконец-то завяжет и с корточек встанет, помедля,
И пойдет по делам по каким позабыл от тоски
Вообще и конкретной тоски, это - зрелище не для
Слабонервных. А я эту муку люблю, однолюб.
Во дворах воробьев хороня, мы ее предвкушали,
И - пожалуйста. "Стар я, - бормочет, - несчастлив и глуп.
Вы читали меня в периодике?" Нет, не читали
И читать не намерены. Каждый и сам умудрен
Километрами шизофрении на страшном диване.
Кто избавился, баловень, от роковых шестерен?
(Поступь рока слышна у Набокова в каждом романе.)
Раз в Тбилиси весной в ореоле своем голубом
Знаменитость, покойная ныне, кумир киноведов,
Приложением к лагерным россказням вынес альбом -
Фотографии кровосмесителей и людоедов.
На пол наискось выскользнул случаем с пыльных страниц
Позитив в пол-ладони, окутанный в чудную дымку
Простодушия, что ли, сияния из-под ресниц …
- Мне здесь пять, - брякнул гений. Мы отдали должное снимку.
Как тебе наше сборище, а, херувим на горшке?
Люб тебе пожилой извращенец, косеющий с первой?
Это было похлеще историй о тухлой кишке
И о взломе мохнатого сейфа. Опять-таки нервы.
В свете вышеизложенного, башковитый тростник,
Вряд ли ты ошарашишь читателя своеобразьем
И премудростью книжною. Что же касается книг,
Человека воде уподобили, пролитой наземь,
Во Второй Книге Царств. Он умрет, как у них повелось.
Воробьи (да, те самые) сядут знакомцу на плечи.
Если жизнь дар и вправду, о смысле не может быть речи.
Разговор о Великом Авось.

1991

✧✧✧

When a middle-aged man, turning red, finally finishes
Tying his laces, he stands up and lingers, until
He goes about his business, forgetting what it is
Out of general sorrow and a concrete grief—this is not a spectacle
For the weak of heart. This pain is my one true love.
Once we anticipated it, burying dead sparrows in the yard,
And voila: "I'm old," he mutters, "unhappy and foolish.
Have you read my stuff in that journal?" No, we haven't
And we won't either, when without it each is wise
From miles of dementia on a tormenting divan.
Is anyone saved, naughty child, from the gears of fate?
Fate's footstep, audible in every Nabokov novel.

One spring in Tbilisi, in a lavender halo,
The celebrity (an idol of cinematographers, now dead)
Brought out an album to supplement his gulag tales,
Photographs of incestors and cannibals.
But suddenly a half-seen picture—shrouded in the haze
Of candidness radiant under eyelashes—
Slipped from dusty pages, aslant, to the ground.
"I was only five," the genius blurted. We admired it.
What do you think of us, cherub on a chamberpot?
Is the old pervert dear to you, drunk on one vodka shot?
It was more wrenching than your stories of the fragrant anus
And breaking into the pubic safe. Your heart again.
In light of what's been said, you feeble reed,
You hardly strike your readers dumb with original
Or bookish wisdom. And speaking of books,
In Second Kings, a man is compared to water
Spilled on the ground. Which means he'll die, as is the custom.
Sparrows—yes, those very sparrows—perch on the shoulder
          of their acquaintance.
If life really is a gift, one shouldn't speak of meaning—
It's a matter of the Great Perhaps.

Все громко тикает. Под спичечные марши
В одежде лечь поверх постельного белья.
Ну-ну, без глупостей. Но чувство страха старше
И долговечнее тебя, душа моя.
На стуле в пепельнице теплится окурок,
И в зимнем сумраке мерцают два ключа.
Вот это смерть и есть, допрыгался, придурок?
Жердь, круговерть и твердь - мученье рифмача …
Нагая женщина тогда встает с постели
И через голову просторный балахон
Наденет медленно, и обойдет без цели
Жилище праздное, где память о плохом
Или совсем плохом. Перед большой разлукой
Обычай требует ненадолго присесть,
Присядет и она, не проронив ни звука.
Отцы, учители, вот это - ад и есть!
В прозрачной темноте пройдет до самой двери,
С порога бросит взгляд на жалкую кровать,
И пальцем странный сон на пыльном секретере
Запишет, уходя, но слов не разобрать.

1994

To My Wife

A loud ticking, everywhere. The rhythmic march
Of matches jostling in a pocket. I lie on the bed,
Fully dressed. Relax, it's nothing. But the feeling of terror
Is more ancient and more durable than you, my soul.
On the chair, an ashtray gleams with cigarette butts.
Against winter twilight, two keys glimmer.
This is death: you're really in it now, idiot.
Pedestal, cycle, pebble—the rhymer's torture.
A naked woman now rises from the bed
And slowly slips over her head a roomy
Gown, then aimlessly walks around
The bare dwelling, full of a bad memory
Or one worse than that. Before a great parting
Custom demands that you sit a few moments,
And she sits down, not breathing a sound.
Fathers, Teachers, look—hell exists.
She walks to the door in transparent dark,
At the threshold casts a glance at the wretched bed,
Then traces a strange dream on the dusty desk
As she leaves—words you can't understand.

The Use of Poetry
Sergey Gandlevsky

A prize for poetry can baffle its recipient—when a private thing, a personal predilection that's almost a whim, is rewarded. It's as if an inveterate mushroom-hunter or lover of ice fishing were given a prize. It's customary to think that there are all kinds of whims but poetry is a serious and hardly useless pastime. Yet in the last twenty years, many (and certainly the best) Russian poets have recoiled from the word "use." Like little children, poets demand that they be loved for no other reason than that they exist.

Society is correct to treat poetry with seriousness, but poetry is also correct to hold onto the bulwark of its own uselessness.

It's good to sit in the hot sun on the grass and look at a river. But the supposition that the sun, the plants, and water have the goal and purpose of giving us pleasure hardly enters the healthy mind; about the meaning of nature we can only guess—each person is remitted a certain amount of imagination, intelligence, and temperament. Such is poetry: its ultimate direct aspirations are unclear and mysterious; the impressions that it produces are only the indirect consequences of its existence.

We can hope that poetry will help us, but we cannot demand help from it. Poetry is a gift, not a salary. Only when we finally take into account, when we get used to the idea that the natural responsibility of poetry is to be poetry, it is conceivable, I think, to fold down your fingers and estimate whether poetry has any earthly task. Not insisting especially on anything, I'll offer a few thoughts.

First. Occupied primarily by words and by himself, the poet day in and day out writes his ideal self-portrait, personifies on the page a dream about himself. The tactical allegory "lyrical hero" we should understand in its original meaning—the poet "heroizes" himself, displays the most vivid attributes of his personality, subdued in daily life by routine conflict. A constant contact with the ideal twin disciplines the author, helps him not to give up. The author feels that the gap is too wide between himself and the lyrical hero—it's disastrous for both: the devastation responds as muteness in the best instance, and in the worst, idle chatter.

But the moral return from creativity is known not only to those who write; readers feel it as well.

Poetry relates to reality like a finished manuscript to a rough draft. Art didn't invent the drama of life. The drama is in the nature of things, but things obscure it. Poetry focuses life to a sharp clarity, and the main celebratory foundation of existence becomes visible from everyday babble. Poetry is the subjunctive mood of life, to remember how we would be, if we were not.... In short, poetry is in a position to better our morals.

Second. Everyone knows that life is not sugar; loneliness is perhaps the most bitter of its burdens. A person often cannot share his despondency, his sudden thoughts, his good moods, but he opens a book, and he's somehow not alone. It turns out that total strangers were already here, were thinking, were happy or angry like he was, and for the same reason that he is. Suddenly, these people are no longer strange to him. That revealed spiritual likeness bothers the teenager's feelings of his own exclusivity, but soon enough we become adults and have it up to here with our own exclusivity. In other words, art is also a communication. And poetry is the best means of communication, because it's the most emotional.

And third. Coffee boils over on the stove just as if it's trying to put its head through a sweater; the Russian word "train" [poezd] is already preparation for "delay" [opozdanie]; after a twenty-year intermission, the old forgotten poet appears in public in a sport coat, buttoned enthusiastically in the wrong hole. This is all the costly small change of the world, in which we for some reason awaken once and for the last time. It is shameful to be hard of hearing and half-blind. If only inattention to our small creativity, not to say anything about apathy toward Creation, or the ailment of mechanical existence offended us more than profanity! Poetry can help us to value life. Even when a poet curses the universe, he has nevertheless noticed it; it has genuinely disturbed him. "Keen observation," Mandelstam said, "is the virtue of the lyrical poet." I dare to add that keen observation is a kind of gratefulness. Poetry, in the end, is always the artless gratitude to the world for the fact of existence.

1997

Notes

Translating a poet as allusive as Gandlevsky inevitably requires some annotation, but I've tried to balance tonal continuity against the experience of textual blockage. At times, I have dropped specific cultural references when context is already firmly established; for example, I dropped the moniker of "KVN" in favor of the more general "TV," knowing that the "bulbous eye" shape would imply some distinct, early kind of television. At other times, I leave the particular reference—like the reference to "Bonny M," an East German pop band—when such references are themselves ephemeral and probably opaque even to a Russian reader of a younger generation. Thanks to Sergey Gandlevsky and Dmitry Psurtev in particular for their help.

Stanzas

The "upas" to which Gandlevsky refers is in Alexander Pushkin's poem, "The Upas," about a mythical poison tree used by a lord to poison his enemies; however, the servant died while transporting the poison to his lord. This poem was typically part of the grade school syllabus and part of the Soviet ideological system.

"The pane that mama washed" is a phrase often used by Russian spelling books to teach letters.

The section about the "charlatan" borrows from Pushkin's "To the Poet," which argues the poet is holy, his work sacred. The image of the "staff" or "tripod" is adopted from the Hebrew Scriptures as a Mosaic instrument of power (and from the classical Oracle of Delphi), then by Pushkin, later by Khodasevich.

"Where one needs spirits to be happy" alludes to Prince Vladimir's rationale for choosing Christianity (over Islam, in this case) as the state religion for ancient Rus', because Christianity did not prohibit alcohol.

Sergey Esenin, an early twentieth century Russian poet, was beloved for his folk style. Andre Chenier, the greatest French poet of the 18th century, widely translated by Pushkin and Lermontov, was executed during the Terror. Both poets are often remembered as persecuted geniuses.

December 1977

"Oka" is a river in western Russia, the largest right-bank tributary of the Volga. "Sheksna" is a river in northwest Russia, connecting the Volga and the Baltics. "Pripyat" is a river that originates in the Ukraine and flows into the Dniper.

"There are nights when grass staggers under..."
"I'm alive ..." echoes Osip Mandelstam's "To Marina Tsvetaeva."

"Old Arbat" is a neighborhood in Moscow renowned for having retained its pre-Revolutionary architecture.

"Twice, last night, I dreamt..."
This poem echoes the dream-like quality of Blok's "Free Thoughts" poems.

The "Victory" was a car manufactured in the Soviet Union after World War II.

"Briullov's lilac dusk" refers to the Russian artist Karl Briullov's masterwork, the apocalyptic painting *The Last Day of Pompeii*.

The octagon, in Euclidean thought, is a symbol of air.

"I'll kiss..."
"Terek" is a river that flows from the Caucasus mountains in Georgia through Vladikavkaz, into the Caspian Sea.

"Vladikavkaz" is the capital of North Ossetia-Alania, founded during the Russian conquest of the Caucasus.

"Tbilisi" is the capital of Georgia. Avlabar and Okrakany are suburbs of Tbilisi.

"Long ago, we wandered in on the festival of death..."
"Prince Andrei on the battlefield of Austerlitz" refers to a crucial scene in Lev Tolstoy's *War and Peace* in which the prince experiences a revelation that the immense sky, in its peaceful splendor, outweighs all human actions.

"Look, it's snowing again. There are words in Russian..."
The unshot gun is clearly a reference to Chekhov's famous words that the gun that hangs on the wall in the first act will be shot by the third act.

"Here rivers cry like a patient under the knife..."
Gandlevsky refers to a specific vacation spot; Alushta is a resort in the Crimea on the Black Sea, where all the accoutrements of civilization are available.

Gandlevsky refers to the "arba," a kind of cart used in the Crimea and Caucasus. In these lines, Sergey alludes to a scene from Alexander Pushkin's *Travel to Arzrum*, where Pushkin writes about climbing down a mountain slope; seeing a cart carry what looks like a coffin dragged by a pair of oxen, Pushkin asks the cart-puller what he's carrying. "Griboyed" was the laconic answer. Alexander Sergeevich (also Pushkin's first and patronymic names) Griboyedov, another tragic poet and ambassador to Persia, was killed by zealots during a siege of the embassy. The story of his life and work is recounted in Yuri Tynyanov's *The Death of Vazir-Mukhtar*.

The Pamir, also known as "The Roof of the World," is a mountain range in Tadjikistan and Kirgistan.

"Suvorov" was the great 19th century Russian general who, crossing the Alps, defeated Austria and liberated Italy.

"Surikov" is the famous 19th century Russian painter of the "peredvizhniki" school, whose immense painting *Suvorov crossing the Alps* depicts the mighty Russian General Suvorov leading his troops to victory—sliding down the mountain on their behinds to meet their opponents.

The "Vanch" is a river in the Pamir mountains.

To My Mother
"Mozhaika" is a region in Moscow where Gandlevsky grew up, populated by communal apartment buildings known as "kommunalkas."

The television to which Gandlevsky refers is the "KVN," the first Soviet model, which had an unusually convex surface.

"Holy Iness" is a reference to a painting by the Spanish painter Ribera (1591-1652).

"A picture of this world, dear to the mind..."
Gandlevsky's prose-poem is actually rhymed iambic pentameter in Russian.

The "mute giant" refers to a famous story by Ivan Turgenev about a mute serf forced to kill his dog Mumu at the behest of his master.

"Germann" is the main character in Pushkin's short story "Queen of Spades."

"Dear God, allow me to recall my works..."
"Camp M.E.I." is a camp organized by Moscow Energy Institute.

"Be Prepared," in Russian, "Budst gotov!" was Lenin's slogan for preparedness, now mocked for its militarism and false promises.

"Merry-Go-Round" is a slight deviation from Gandlevsky's "Ferris Wheel," which in Russian translates literally as "circle of view."

"Omsk to Osh" measures the breadth of the former U.S.S.R., from Siberia to Kirgistan, with the circular wonder of the "O" sounds.

"Simonov" was an infamous Soviet poet, whose famous poem about WWII is quoted in the next line: "Do you remember, Alyosha?"

The "Enchanted Traveler" is a reference to Nikolay Leskov's book of the same title.

"Pamir" is a mountain range, but here Gandlevsky refers to the brand of cheap Soviet cigarettes that depict a shadowy figure on a mountaintop, perhaps not unlike the Marlboro Man.

"Shostkino" is a Soviet movie studio, whose films are disintegrating on poor negatives.

"Struck down with this illness..."
"Sad demon" may be a reference to Lermontov's famous poem, and "African passion" may refer to Pushkin, whose grandfather was an African "given" to Peter the Great.

"Alcoholism..." is appropriation of a line by Vladimir Solovyov, the poet and philosopher, who wrote "Panmongolism, though its name is wild...".

With "Ms. Swaggers-in-a-glass jacket" Gandlevsky further corrupts the slang reference for alcohol, "girlfriend in a glass jacket."

"Here is our street, let's say..."
The fourteen-line stanza is in imitation of Pushkin.

"Ordzhonikidzerzhinsky" is an ascerbic conflation of the names of two Soviet revolutionary heroes, Ordzhonikidze and Felix Dzerzhinsky, whose statue was summarily upended by protesting crowds during the 1991 coup of Gorbachev.

"Drugstore, line of folks, shiner" echoes Alexander Blok's poem, which begins "Night, drugstore, street, lamp."

"Today it's my turn" is a quote from Alexander Pushkin's *Eugene Onegin*.

"Okudzhava," or Bulat Okudzhava, is the folk guitarist and poet who sings ballads; sentimental hero of intellectuals.

"Drevlan" were the people killed (by pigeons who carried flaming straw) by Olga in vengeance for the murder of her son in early Rus'.

"Geography" is a game played by children to name towns.

"Chita, Suchan, Karaganda" are Soviet concentration camps; Mandelstam died in Suchan.

"The chatter of daws in the autumn yard..."
"The gutteral refrain" actually refers to the "burring" speech impediment (the inability to say "r" or "l") that afflicted Lenin.

"To O.E."
"Batumi" is a city on the shore of the Black Sea, now part of Georgia.

"Chorny, Grechaninov, Gedike, and Glinka" are composers whose musical exercises are popular for young students of piano.

"...Archilas, Givis, and Natelas..." are typical Georgian names, in the plural.

"Admiral Nakhimov" is a huge ocean liner, which sank a few years after this poem was written.

"The communal zoo has quieted..."
The Soviet policy of collectivizing extended even to living arrangements, where multiple families shared cramped apartments with a single kitchen. Joseph Brodsky writes of this experience in "A Room and a Half," from *Less than One* (Farrar, Straus, & Giroux).

"*Three Musky Tears*" is how Gandlevsky misheard "The Three Musketeers" as a child.

"Kataev" was a Soviet writer who was allowed to publish his memoirs of Esenin, Mandelstam, Mayakovsky and other poets; the memoirs are "artistic, but sentimental" and often overemphasize the author's importance to literature, "giving these famous poets nicknames so that we all had to guess who he meant, and we didn't have other sources of information so it really pissed us off" (Psurtsev).

"The twilight came late. A blanket..."
"Boney M" is a group of black East German singers, in vogue during the seventies.

"Carmen" is a Soviet perfume.

"Generalissimo" is Stalin.

"In the beginning of December, where nature dreams..."
"Sailor's Silence" is the name of the hospital, which Gandlevsky mentions is near one of the jails in Moscow, and had a reputation something like Bedlam.

"The lynch-law of sudden maturity..."
The "custom in Russian poetry/ Of breaking mirrors" particularly refers to Sergey Esenin's poem "The Black Man."

To Dmitry Prigov
Dmitry Prigov is an avant-garde artist and "textmaker" whose work with Soviet myths clearly influences this poem.

"Rehab" actually refers to a special type of Soviet clinic where one is rehabilitated from alcohol without consent, and under prison-like conditions.

Elegy
"Who's in the U.S., who suffering in Komi/ As the poet Sadi said sometime before" is another adoption from Pushkin's *Eugene Onegin*. In the final stanza, Pushkin wonders where his friends have gone:

> But those to whom, as friends and brothers,
> My first few stanzas I once read—

'Some are no more, and distant others'
As Sadi long before us said.
                    (James E. Falen, 1995).

In light of these lines, Gandlevsky's appropriation implies that those who have emigrated to the United States no longer exist, an idea that comes up in the next poem.

"Sadi" is a 13th century Persian poet.

To Bakhyt Kenjeev
Bakhyt Kenjeev is a Russian poet from Kazakhstan who emigrated to Canada.

The first stanza's custom ceremony refers to the Soviet Union's blackballing émigré achievements.

The line "'sheep rhymes with 'ship'" is more humorous in Russian, because the words in Russian do not rhyme, and force the reader to guess the English rhyme.

"Doctor Spock" wrote the best-selling guide to child-rearing, and transformed Soviet parenting in the 1960s.

"The repeating theme" is a quote taken from Pushkin's *Mozart and Salieri*.

"Karelia" is a republic northeast of Petersburg; the lake referred to here is likely Lake Onega.

"Oh, the lilacs this May!..."
This poem is written in imitation of Russian translations of classical hexameter verse.

"To land a job at the garage..."
The "black pistol" refers to a folk song called "Bolshoy Karetny" by the singer Vladimir Vysotsky, whose refrain goes: "where are your seventeen years?/On Bolshoi Karetny./Where are your seventeen misfortunes?/On Bolshoi Karetny./Where is your black pistol?/On Bolshoi Karetny./Where are you not anymore?/On Bolshoi Karetny."

"Gazli" is a small town in Uzbekistan and "Kaluga" is a town in central Russia.

To Aleksey Magarik

Aleksey Magarik is a friend of the poet and a musician who wrote many gulag songs.

"Kostroma" is an ancient Russian city, part of the Golden Ring around Moscow.

"Velikie Luki" is an ancient Russian city west of Moscow.

The gulag town that Gandlevsky refers to is "Vorkuta."

To Pavel Movchan
Pavel Movchan is a Ukranian nationalist poet and a friend of Gandlevsky's.

"Kresti" is the infamous prison in Petersburg.

These lines may echo a famous Esenin poem: "In that land where yellow nettles grow ... They are all murderers and thieves/ Just as their fate made them/ And I came to love their sad stares and their socketed cheeks."

"Muzhik" has historically meant "peasant" in Russian, but has come to mean any man.

Here, the "starlet" is an abstraction of Gandlevsky's particular pinup, Natalya Gundareva, a Soviet movie star whose image was that of the quintessential Russian woman: good wife, mother, large sensuous body, etc. (Psurtsev).

Camille Corot was the French genre painter from the 19th century who painted "Gust of Wind."

"*The prophesied final solo*" is the trumpet referred to in the Book of Revelation, 8:10-11. Gandlevsky here alludes to the sinister irony that "chernobyl," in Ukrainian, actually means "wormwood"; many people took the nuclear disaster at Chernobyl as a sign that the end of the world was at hand.

"Semyon Kosikh, drunk since May-Day..."
"Semyon Kosikh" is a humorous name in Russian, likely drawn from the Siberian or Uralian last names—"kosoy" is slang for being drunk.

"More light" is likely the last thing said by Goethe on his deathbed.

The "foil tooth" refers to the "criminal class" style of dressing a tooth in metal foil to appear more wealthy.

"All the lines began with 'and'"—A stylistic device that echoes the Biblical style, and thus carries the weight of traditional Russian poetry.

"Opened my barbarian mouth" alludes to the famous Pushkin poem, "The Prophet." The angel in Pushkin gives to the poet the gift of prophesy and ardent speech, but only after he tears out the poet's tongue and replaces it with a snake's.

These three lines allude to Pushkin's "Conversation Between the Poet, the Critic and the Reader," wherein the poet proclaims the power of imagination and sneers above the crowd, while the other two offer their legitimate counter-arguments.

Gandlevsky writes "Nikulin, Vitsin, Morgunov." They may be described as the Russian Marx brothers, hence my translation. These lines also allude to the popular anecdote that describes a loyal husband returning to his home, where his wife busily hides her lovers wherever she can.

"When a middle-aged man, turning red, finally finishes..."
The celebrity filmmaker is Sergei Paradzhanov, an aesthete with a love of the perverse.

"The fragrant anus" and "breaking into the pubic safe" are slang for homosexual and heterosexual intercourse, probably rape.

"Feeble reed" is lifted from Pascal: "Man is only a reed, the feeblest reed in nature, but he is a thinking reed."

The "Great Perhaps" echoes Rabelais.

To My Wife
Gandlevsky writes more directly about his brain surgery in his memoir, *Trepanation of the Skull.*

IN THE GRIP OF STRANGE THOUGHTS: RUSSIAN POETRY IN A NEW ERA

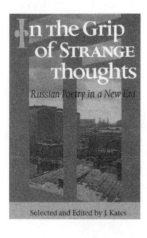

◆ 118 POEMS BY 32 CONTEMPORARY
    RUSSIAN POETS

◆ BILINGUAL (RUSSIAN & ENGLISH)
    ON FACING PAGES

◆ FOREWORD BY POET AND CRITIC
    MIKHAIL AIZENBERG

◆ INTRODUCTION AND
    AFTERWORD BY J. KATES

◆ BIOGRAPHICAL NOTES ON POETS
    AND TRANSLATORS

444 PAGES
0-939010-5-69 19.95 PAPER
0-939010-5-77 30.00 CLOTH

"...an enjoyable and admirable work. Its thirty-two poets show a tremendous thematic and stylistic range, but are united in their feeling for the vitality of language."
—*The Times Literary Supplement*

"This book is an absolute gift to students and to lovers of poetry" —*British East-West Journal*

ZEPHYR PRESS
617.713.2813 PHONE & FAX
EDITOR@ZEPHYRPRESS.ORG
WWW.ZEPHYRPRESS.ORG

Other titles from the series

IN THE GRIP OF STRANGE THOUGHTS

SALUTE TO SINGING

Gennady Aygi

Translated by Peter France

These variations on folkloric themes are born out of the Chuvash and Turkic motifs that Aygi grew up with, and which Aygi and France have collected in their work on Chuvash poetry. A Turkic language, Chuvash is spoken by about a million and a half people in and around Chuvashia—formerly an autonomous republic of the USSR—located 500 miles east of Moscow. Now in his 60s, Aygi continues to be celebrated as the Chuvash national poet, and as a major poet of the Russian language.

"Peter France's scrupulous versions are faithful not simply to the often ambiguous sense of the originals, but also to the typographical minutiae ... which spell out the exclamations, questionings, pauses, vulnerabilities and praises of this most remarkable poet."
—TIMES LITERARY SUPPLEMENT

Poetry / 96 pages
Paper (0-939010-69-0) $12.95

THE SCORE OF THE GAME

Tatiana Shcherbina

Translated by J Kates

Shcherbina emerged in the early 1980s as a spokesperson for the new, independent Moscow culture. Her work was first published in the official press of the Soviet Union in 1986, and five volumes of her poetry were published in samizdat prior to 1990. Her poetry is now widely published in both established and experimental journals at home and abroad, and has been translated into Dutch, German, French, and English. Shcherbina's poetry blends the personal with the political, and the source for her material is pulled from classical literature, as well as French and German cultural influences.

Poetry / 136 pages
Paper (0-939010-70-4) $12.95

A MILLION PREMONITIONS

Viktor Sosnora

Translated by Mark Halperin and Dinara Georgeoliani

Viktor Sosnora has been one of the most consistently experimental of Russian poets since he began writing in the 1960s. Reaching back as far as medieval Rus' and as far forward as metrical and linguistic innovation permit, he has written with a voice unique and wide-ranging. Historical allusion, conscious anachronism, humor and intensity of word-play dominate by turns Sosnora's continually protean poetry.

Poetry / 144 pages
Paper (0-939010-76-3) $12.95